Weird Foods of Portugal

Adventures of an Expat

Wendy Lee Hermance

Also by Wendy Hermance

What's that Stuff? A Natural Foods Reference Guide

Where I'm Going With this Poem - Selected Poems

The Mizzou International Directory (Editor)

WENDY LEE HERMANCE

Weird Foods of Portugal
Adventures of an Expat

www.wendyleehermance.com

Copyright © 2022 Wendy Lee Hermance
All rights reserved.

Paperback ISBN 978-1-7346044-3-6

All rights reserved. No part of this book may be reproduced in any form or by any means without prior written permission from the author except for brief quotations embodied in critical essay, article or review. These articles and/or review must state the correct title and contributing authors of this book by name.

Book design and layout: Rachel Bostwick

Portuguese editor: Sónia Cascais Sá

Illustrations: Channarong Pherngjanda

Photo of Joana Vasconcelos: Cláudia Rodrigues

Back cover photo: Lily Auyong

Cover art and design: The Oleocalligraphy Collective

Praise

"With her typically American intrepidness, her thirst for a good story and her power of observation, Hermance closes-in on the Portuguese she encounters along the way, bringing to us a psychological picture of the Portuguese individual and society that you won´t find on expat guides. Lastly, her unusual grasp for "Portuguese quaintness" also makes this book worth buying." – David Peres Rebelo

"I´m flattered. I think! – Dave Barry, *Best. State. Ever.: A Florida Man Defends His Homeland*

"The book is a great combination of lyrical, beautiful prose with the writer's personality threaded throughout.... The reader is jarred by the dreamlike, erotic quality and fanciful descriptions of *António's Stick*, for example. I think the book is witty and lyrical and accomplishes a good mix of social commentary and beautiful descriptions of Portugal and its people."
 - Sara Thwaite, Editor, *Boys in the Trees, a Memoir* (Carly Simon), *Julie Taboulie's Lebanese Kitchen*, (Julie Ann Sageer)

"Fascinating and real. You bring the reader to the place that you are writing about." - Dawn McCormack
I read it in two sittings and now I feel I know something of your outlook which I appreciate as brilliant, full of color, place, imagination and wisdom....Your work

expands my mind in how approaching living and writing can be done with more freedom to cherish your individuality and appreciate the grief as well as the beauty in life. - Anne Stackpole-Cuellar, *Fidelia's Friends*, and *On the Wing* (CD)

"Wendy Lee Hermance's prose and poetry are made of touching and surprising childhood memories – of shriveled apples, old pillows, fallen tree limbs, imaginary radio stations and things so difficult to put into words that we can only glimpse them between the lines of this highly compelling work."
 - Richard Zimler, *The Last Kabbalist of Lisbon, The Warsaw Anagrams, The Lost Gospel of Lazarus*

"The prose and poetry in Wendy Lee Hermance's personal narrative comprise a unique memoir beginning with richly detailed childhood experiences, moving through adolescence, ultimately manifesting in adulthood. *Where I'm Going with this Poem*, is a hymn to "this lovely human mess" that is the speaker's life, but this is a life filled with a myriad of experiences, all described with a poet's empathy and attention to detail reminding us all, as Hermance did in the last poem of the collection, of our capacity to *find some things to love*". - Marjory Wentworth, NYTs Best-Selling author, *Out of Wonder, Poems Celebrating Poets*

TABLE OF CONTENTS

Weird Foods of Portugal .... *i*
A Glossary of Portuguese Words for English Speakers 1
You Are Every Time Welcome in Bulgaria 3
Hello, Dog! 43
Weird Foods of Portugal 83
Happiness Factory 101
A Secret Soldier 141
I Brined A Turkey 175
I Wonder As I Wander 205
António's Stick 229
The Portuguese Model of Physiotherapy 239
Francelos 283
Love in the Air 295
Portugal, On My Word 329
Beijinhos 333
Further Reading 336

Portugal

....if only you were just salt, sun, the south,

the shrewd sparrow,

the meek colloquial ox,

the sizzling sardine,

the waddling fishwife,

the scribbler bundled up in pretty adjectives,

the silent, almondish complaint

of sharp eyes with black lashes,

if only you were just the buzzing of summer, the

buzz of fashion,

the decrepit asthmatic dog of beaches,

the caged cricket, the cagey customer,

the calendar on the wall, the pin on a lapel,

if only, Portugal, you were just three syllables....

Excerpt Alexandre O'Neill, "Portugal," © Translation: 1997, Richard Zenith

A Glossary of Portuguese Words for English Speakers

If you like bread, ham, and cheese, and know only these few additional words you will never go hungry, nor be shabbily furnished in Portugal.

Abacate—Avocado. Grown in many varieties up to the size of papayas. Eaten with cinnamon (*canela*) and sugar, many locals do not like avocados, and not even with lemon, garlic and salt – which are all normal seasonings around here. This is Guacamole Heaven!

Advogados—Attorneys. Usually smelling better than *bacalau*, but they are far more hazardous than tiny, choking fish bones. Similar to US varieties. Best used as fertilizer.

A GLOSSARY OF PORTUGUESE WORDS

Aipo—Celery. Considered so offensively strong flavored that the word is not spoken in polite company. *Alho* (garlic) is a sweet word.

Alcachofra—Artichoke. Frozen *coração de alcachofra* are available at low cost in every grocery store, but oddly, fresh are almost never found despite the thistle being used to curdle a soft Portuguese cheese. (*Almofada* is pillow).

Alfândega – Government Customs, which may determine tariffs on imported goods based on the weather, or the quality of the lunch served that day. Given an unfair reputation by certain multi-national shipping companies that try to bribe recipients for added fees falsely blaming the *Alfândega*. (*Almôndega* is Meatball).

Alheira - Sausage of bread and smoke flavoring. This was historically made by Jewish people pretending to be pork eaters to evade the Inquisitions. Today *alheira* may contain any variety of meat products including pork.

Almoço- A strictly-observed religious ceremony performed daily, also known as lunch. *Pequeno-Almoço* = Breakfast involves less ceremony as it is only one piece of bread.

Ananás—Pineapple. Pronounced, "Anna Nash." How this woman got a tropical fruit named after her when she doesn't even sound French is a mystery. (See *Francesinha,* and *Reineta).*

Atum—Tuna. Invented in Portugal by *Conservas Ramirez,* operating continuously in Matosinhos since 1853 is the now-standard ring-pull can.

A GLOSSARY OF PORTUGUESE WORDS

Azeitonas—Olives. *Azeite*—Olive oil. Portuguese olive oil was shipped around the world in clay vessels before the time of Christ.

Bacalau—Odiferous, salt-crusted sleds blocking store aisles October-May. Traditionally this was dry-salted, and sun/air dried Atlantic cod caught north of Portugal, (Iceland, Norway and New Foundland) until fished to near-extinction. Now other fish frozen first, injected with salt solution, are sold as *bacalau*. Norwegian *klipfish* is closest to the original. Fascinating history; it just tastes rotten to me.

Bifana—Not beef (*bife*), but pork, (*porco*) thinly sliced, cooked slowly in beer, hot peppers, and garlic, and laid into a chewy, white roll. Similar to northern Carolina spicy peppers and vinegar pulled pork sandwiches.

Bombeiro—Firefighter. The essential phone number to keep handy if you are a multitasking cook, like some idiots (OK; me) is "1-1-2." Lovely people.

Bolo de Caca—Sweetish, griddle-cooked yeast rolls like English crumpets we called *English muffins* in the US. Originating on Madeira Island, great as burger buns.

Broa—Brick-like bread of cornmeal (*milho*) when re-served as a *couvert* appetizer, delightfully nutty-flavored when fresh. Used in *bacalhau* casseroles made with cream.

Cappuccino—Avoid oversweet, instant Nestlé's by ordering *uma Meia de Leite* at 1/3 the price. Or, ask for "*uma Americano-com leite caliente, sem acugar, com chocolate,*" like I do, in which case you will be handed a plain espresso for being a smarty-pants, or else asked in impeccable English, "Do you

A GLOSSARY OF PORTUGUESE WORDS

mean that you want a *cappuccino?"* Whipped cream is called *chantily*.

Carne—Meat. Also, women's undergarments color called *blush* or *nude* in less frank places.

Chu Chu—Pale green squashes shaped like poodle's heads, with whiskers to match. One must risk self-harm with a sharp knife, trimming the slippery, lumpy rind with its whiskers -which never softens no matter how long you boil before blending it into soup. *Why?*

Couvert—Appetizer. Possibly rejected by other diners before you, usually *broa*, olives, and maybe a bit of tuna pâté. Portuguese meals are so generous that a *couvert* and its small added cost may be unnecessary. Most cafés will serve individual snacks of olives (*azeitonas*), nuts (*noz*), bread, (*pão*), cheese, (*queijo*) and (*tremoços*) on request. *Tremoços* (lupini beans) are 36% protein. You always have to ask for butter (*manteiga*).

Cogumelos—Mushrooms. Every kind are available here fresh, and in low-cost frozen mixes handy for adding umami, especially to vegetarian cooking.

Estofador—Portugal has bullfights. *Estofadors* wear *monteras, toreador* pants, capes, when confronting bulls with pinking shears. (*Estafodors* are really upholsterers.)

Feira—Every day except maybe Sunday a *feira* is happening somewhere near you. At these wondrous bazaars shoes, pajamas, baskets, bed sheets, underwear - the color of carne - fabrics, flowers, live rabbits, fish, live chickens, hardware - anything and everything one could possibly need may be found. The highest-quality Portuguese goods made for international export

A GLOSSARY OF PORTUGUESE WORDS

are often found at *feiras,* sold for pennies on the euro with tiny flaws. The *Feiras Tradicionais de Portugal* website posts schedules.

Fiambre—Ham. There are so many varieties it's just not worth going into here.

Francesinha - A layered, gravy-ladled, meat-redundant, runny-egg hot mess on a plate. (See the story, "Weird Foods of Portugal.")

Frango—Chicken. *Churrasqueira* is BBQ. The *frango* will be thoughtfully cut up into hand-sized pieces very rapidly, so if preferred whole, you must speak up quickly. Conversely, pizzas are rarely cut up without asking.

Frigorífico —Fantastic! Marvelous! (At present this word just means "Refrigerator," but it´s such an underused, and great word I´m trying to popularize it for more frequent use. For some reason this hasn't really caught on yet.)

Frutaria—Beloved neighborhood fruit and vegetable shops with produce possibly grown by the shopkeeper's family. They also sell household essentials. During the the pandemic, when local governments were struggling to keep people safe following conflicting policies set by non-elected, self-interested, non-scientists outside their borders, and stay at home mandates were imposed, *frutarias* kept Portugal fed and cared for. Mad Respect!

Horta—Vegetable garden, or garden shop. *Peixinhos da horta*, "little fish in the garden" are tempura green beans Portuguese brought to Japan along with the word for thank you, *obrigada*. (Before Portuguese sailors arrived, Japan had neither cuisine nor courtesy).

A GLOSSARY OF PORTUGUESE WORDS

Janela—Window. Portugal has so few official girl's names I'm trying to popularize *Janela* to give *Patrícia, Joanna, Cristina, Susana, Ana, Cláudia, Teresa,* and *Maria* a rest. For some reason, this hasn't really caught on yet.

K—*OK* is *OK.* Slangy American-English words are popular in business and product names and advertising.

Lã—Wool. Lamb (*cordeiro*) is not so commonly eaten here, but goat (*chanfana*) is. (Is it used in pet food, which costs here more than the highest quality meat for human consumption?)

Legumes—Vegetables. Used very sparingly. In one study four out of five burly building contractors became visibly uncomfortable when presented with a dish of tomato, onion, and lettuce for their burgers, calming only when presented with a new platter of plain meat and bread with all traces of vegetable removed. Shoppers loitering near vegetables will quickly recite recipes when asked. Their answers always sound rehearsed, and for dishes I've never seen. This reminds me of another mystery I've been unable to crack: the Portuguese foot. People walk miles over lumpy rocks wearing thin-soled dress shoes. My tenant, Maria de Lurdes is the perfect specimen. At 90 years old she walks miles in moderately high-heeled dress shoes. Her daughter, Susana ignored my request to come and examine her mother's feet, so my new plan is to schedule a "floor inspection," which as a conscientious landlord I must do from time to time, then creep close, grab her mother's foot, inspect it quickly for unusual bone and muscle formations, release it apologising for my clumsiness, and to stop any screaming or talk of calling the police (who I am very fond of in Portugal) I will admire her shoes, and say I'd like to buy a pair for myself. That will never happen. When I go outside on this pavement I encase my feet in the thickest-soled, Portuguese flats I can find. I´m considering adding knee pads to my ensembles, too.

Leite—Milk. *Leite de côco, leite de arroz, leite de soja*—Coconut, rice, and soy milk.

Lixo—Garbage. Pronounced *Lee Shu*. When asked why I buy local and boycott Nestlé products, including Lipton and Danone I say that no Portuguese company I know is engineering mass starvation with global water hogging, *and* clogging animal stomachs with toxic waste. *Lixo,* and also *estúpida* and much, much worse words used liberally in Northern Portugal will help you fit in, especially with the older ladies.

Maçã assada—Baked apple. Hammer in a jaunty stick of cinnamon (*canela*), splash on Port wine, or sugar, or marmalade, and water, plop it in a medium-low oven and bake no longer than eight minutes for sublime simplicity served swimming in its own juices.

Morangos—Strawberries. Flavorful and affordable even when the size of kiwi fruit, which are also grown here.

Massa—Pasta, uncooked dough, or construction paste.

Nata—Individual sweet egg custard tart, or dairy cream.

Ovos—Eggs. If it's edible, and orangey-yellow it is almost certainly made of eggs. (*Olhos* are eyes).

A GLOSSARY OF PORTUGUESE WORDS

Pasta—Paste; either pâté; *pasta de atum*, or wall plaster.

Pavimento - Flooring. This elegant word elevates cursing after shattering a limb or drinking glass on the hard granite and tile floors.

Petiscoes—Tapas. Bite-sized, fried, breaded, or dough-wrapped cakes of minced fish or meat, lovely with a beverage and tangy olives when fresh. Often bought frozen and reheated.

Pipocas—Popcorn. Great for curling up to watch American films shown all the time on regular TV, along with German, Spanish, French and Korean shows, or while watching RTP´s nightly *Joker* game show, which is the how the upper-class British in Portugal learn Portuguese.

WEIRD FOODS OF PORTUGAL

Prato do dia—also known as *Menu diário* - The famously ample, all-inclusive menu of the day, lunch plate, worker's lunch, or blue-plate special.

Puxe—Pull. *Empurre* is Push, (or Press). *Retirar* is Take, (not Return) highway toll tickets.

Quinta - Farm. City folks often have family farms nearby, and if you are nice to them, they may gift you with vegetables, fruits, or eggs.

Reineta—Flat, mottled green apples preferred for making *maçã assada*, French for "little queen." When I asked a male Portuguese friend why so many foods are named after "little French" females, he said the French were considered "wild," compared to the straightlaced Portuguese. His eyes became distant, he mentioned a motorcycle. His wife cleared her

A GLOSSARY OF PORTUGUESE WORDS

throat, and I am still waiting to get him alone to hear the rest of this story.

Russian Salad—(salada russa) Mayonnaise, dotted with flavorless, frozen, diced potatoes, peas, and carrot, but basically mayonnaise.

Salada—Garnish. One or two lettuce leaves, half a slice of unripe tomato, specks of shredded carrot (*cenoura*), moon slivers of onion (*cebola*) with olive oil, vinegar, and salt. Never varying. *Não.* There are no other dressing options.

Sapateira—Crab. Also, a rack for holding shoes, and a shoemaker. (*Sapataria* is shoe shop).

Sardinhas—Sardines. Portugal exported $9.07 million worth of sardines to Spain, France, Canada, and the USA in 2020. Favored fresh, charred over a grill especially on São João Day, the ancient solstice festival celebrated June 23 and 24, when people also smack each other with cartoonish plastic hammers and garlic.

Sopa—Soup. Boiled and pureed without added seasoning. Prepared as if for invalids, slurped down with gusto by everyone, even the most macho men. Nearly always vegan, there may be one slice of *chouriço* on top of *caldo verde*, (which is mostly mashed potatoes.)

Tortilha—A thick, savoury, greasy cake of pre-fried potatoes Spanish in origin. Mexican corn (*milho*) tortillas are only found in large *hipermarkets*. Look for Poco Loco or Old El Paso brands. Wraps, or *rolitas* of wheat *(trigo)* are widely available, including the Mexican Bimbo brand, (which does not sell corn tortillas here).

A GLOSSARY OF PORTUGUESE WORDS

Tripas—Tripe. Stews made with tripe symbolize Portuguese resistance and resourcefulness. They also can be a rare source of vegetables as many contain beans, carrots, and potatoes. *Cozido à portuguesa* has no beans, *à moda do Porto* has white beans, chunks of blood sausage, and roasted pork or young cow on the bone, and *feijoada à transmontane* has red beans. Of course, being stews anything goes.

Uva—Grapes. *Vinho*—Wine. *Tinto;* red wine, *Branco;* white wine, *Verde*; tingly, crisp white wine. I find Douro region reds softer and smooth, and Alentejo reds rough, like Shiraz. I don´t know much more about wine, except to improve it as needed I throw in a few frozen berries – preferably blackberries or raspberries.

Vizinha—Neighbor. Like kisses and family members, neighbors are important, especially in old neighborhoods. It is not common to invite people outside the family into one's home though, so if you are invited in consider yourself lucky.

Wendy—Pronounced "Endy." I don't mind this pronunciation. I was called "Window" for almost one year on my first job by my Corsican employers. But, "Endy" just sounds so *final*.

Xampu—Brazilian Shampoo. Portuguese *Champô;* pronounced "CHampo."

Zé—A nickname for José , also, *O zé-povinho,* "an ordinary Joe" from Raphael Bordallo Pinhero's cartoon character of that name, created around 1875.

A GLOSSARY OF PORTUGUESE WORDS

For a proper introduction to Portuguese words you might look into the online *Priberam Dictionary of the Portuguese Language*. The "Portuguese Cuisine" entry on the Wikipedia website is also interesting to read.

"Quem decide deixar o país, não tem medo do desconhecido. É duro pensar que o que temos não serve.

Ser estrangeiro é onde os fracos não têm vez. Não há tempo para lamentos ou saudade. Abre mão da comodidade, dos almoços de família, dos amigos de infância, para viver longe de quem amam. Torna-se estranho a si próprio. As condições emocionais mudam e é árduo reaprender a lidar com os sentimentos.
Um sentimento sem país no mundo, apela à solidariedade internacional e à diversidade cultural, para aquietar novas guerras."

Filomena Silva Campos,

Um Sentimento sem País no Mundo

"Perhaps, like most of us in a foreign country, he was incapable of placing people, selecting a frame for their picture, as he would at home; therefore all Americans had to be judged in a pretty equal light, and on this basis his companions appeared to be tolerable examples of local colour and national character."

Truman Capote,

Breakfast at Tiffany's

YOU ARE EVERY TIME WELCOME IN BULGARIA

My apartment has no coffee maker, no tea kettle, and no working refrigerator. I begin my days at the hotel sharing the big breakfast buffet with busloads of tourists from other parts of Europe.

Picture a Neo-Brutalist skyscraper like a deep-sea oil derrick, pumping in a vast and choppy grey sea. Its wind waves are chunks of grey granite broken out of the pavement. Cataracted eyes stare impassively over a vacant, desolate stone courtyard from empty shop windows, all their moisture seals broken.

YOU ARE EVERY TIME WELCOME IN BULGARIA

I end my days inside in the lobby. The lobby is decorated in the sophisticated burgundy, beige, hunter green and black of the early 1990s. Above the back alcove is a paper mural of caricature sketches of old Hollywood stars on white in a charcoal effect. W. C. Fields' cigar ash is always poised to spoil the mobster moll pump of doomed Faye Dunaway of *Bonnie and Clyde*.

Across the lobby's beige travertine floor (dotted with malachite green) are twin mahogany bars facing each other. One is the bar where Thursday nights one female vocalist and one male guitar player perform two, twenty-minute sets. On the opposite end is the check-in counter where the ever-efficient night manager, Rita and her small, but capable staff in impeccable navy-blue pencil skirts and slacks outfits for the men print real estate listings that I email them. Rita has instructed the others to watch for my emails. It may not seem like much to you but, this hotel is all I have left to call "home" in the world.

The hotel´s paying guests spend virtually no time at all here except to sleep, so I get the four-star staff almost exclusively to myself. There are no historic wonders, no museums, no music venues, no shopping or restaurants to speak of in this part of town. Each evening Sérgio pulls one of his bar tables over to the alcove wall socket for me so I can charge up my laptop while urgently searching for another accommodation. I depend nightly on Sérgio´s simple dinners – the "wholegrain" skinny baguette smeared with tuna paste, dotted with sliced hard-boiled egg served with a generous pour of plummy, red Douro wine for €4 each night. It´s still very exotic to me, very European. I haven´t tired of it yet. Without my asking by now Sérgio knows to add extra leaf lettuce and tomato to meet my needs for vitamins and fiber.

Some nights I'm invited to join an elderly British tourist couple too potted to venture out into the city. Most nights it's just me Sérgio, Rita, and her staff. I work at the edge of the alcove until exhausted enough to sleep on the rock-hard, fifty-year old mattress in my stuffy apartment. Then, I pack up my computer, it's long, thick charging cord, and the brick-like voltage converter bought at Best Buy, and I trudge through the lumpy courtyard, around the corner, down the alley. I pass the social housing complex, and approach the edge of the sewage pool. I sharpen up, becoming alert for its glint of wetness in the dark to avoid stepping into it. I juggle the keys, try to remember which passcode goes with which key to get past the next door into the apartment, and finally brace myself to enter the fetid, dusty air. I open the door, drop the backpack. I run a bath to bathe away the injustices of the day, and sleep fitfully, tossing often, and making absolutely certain that I am awake and out of the apartment before seven am.

Three weeks earlier I'd arrived in Porto at 9:30 pm from the US. It was a Thursday night. I was lugging three suitcases with everything I thought I might need for three or four months in a strange country. I knew only my Portuguese attorney, a Century 21 real estate agent, two employees of a boutique hotel I'd stayed at in the Porto neighborhood of Cedofeita nine months earlier, and *Tucha*, a woman I'd met when I stopped on the street in Guimarães ares back then to ask for directions. Luftansa inexplicably cancelled flight after flight, sending passengers shuffling from one terminal to another for hours. I'd dragged my three suitcases for a total of twenty-three hours by the time I arrived to see my apartment for the first time.

The agent, Paulo Barros had assured me this apartment he found for me was in a "privileged location." Paulo did not meet me. I would never see him again. Two of his Century 21 colleagues met me. They instructed my taxi driver, Maurício, (who I´d also met nine months earlier), to go to a different address than the one on the apartment lease. We met underground in a vacant, dimly lit parking garage as if exchanging Cold War secrets.

The instant the door to the apartment was opened, my nose twitched. My eyes burned. Black Mold - straight ahead - peeped from all the edges of a garish, orange polyester curtain, thrown up recently, judging from its newness by decades from anything else in the room. The first thing I noticed about the apartment was that it was infected with Black Mold.

A small, elderly matron was at the back of the room weaving between rickety stacks of bric a brac and old furniture, wearing the colorless pencil skirt, blouse, and cardigan uniform of the old-monied. She glanced up perfunctorily with a calculating smile when introduced as the owner, who had "travelled all the way from her home in the Algarve to meet" me, before resuming her task of inventorying the furnishings. As she did, so did I. Dusty baskets, and crocks of plastic plants, stacks of unmatched china, tiny vases of desiccated weeds the color of dung, plastic cherubs - the sort of things underpaid employees or very young children might give to fulfil gift obligations - china teapots too many to count covered every scarred, brown bureau. An additional pain began to build behind my eyes, as my new life in Portugal was spread before me.

A rickety, homemade plywood bookcase precariously listing to one side held a complete set of accounting textbooks from the Salazar era on its sagging top shelf. The small center aisle in the room hosted a competition for the title of "Ugliest Lamp," with chrome floor lamps topped with incongruous burlap or maroon-pleated cloth shades competing with textured white plaster table lamps sponge-daub painted in pea soup green or pastel orange. Mismatched bar stools, small, trip-worthy wooden foot stools, and magazine racks created an obstacle course to any movement. A white, legless foam sofa was backed into a high-backed reddish brown tweed sofa I vaguely recalled as a very young child in the 1960s being advertised as the "Colonial" model by Castro Convertibles with its unforgettable snappy jingle. This monstrosity was jammed up next to a cracked brown vinyl recliner, its flabby arms covered in cigarette burns, and this was jammed against the one double wide window in the whole downstairs which was covered in the orange polyester gauze, framed in Black Mold. There were also three ancient, television sets.

So, the second thing I noticed about the apartment was that it was nothing but a storage dump for a family of indiscriminate hoarders. At some point I realized the three others in this room were probably a family. Nothing but the unloved, the ugly, the used-up, the utterly worthless, and forgotten for decades had been left here. And me. I´d been conned, made to pay six month´s rent in advance, as approved and signed by my attorney as my Power of Attorney, who´d also directed my funds transfer, and by my Century 21 agents. Six months rent in advance, plus a €1,000 damage deposit. I stood marvelling at the wizardry of photography as I had not since brief attempts at internet dating. The photos Paulo sent me made the place look sunny, spacious, and orderly.

Just twenty-one hours before I'd been sleeping in my mid-century modern guesthouse in the Park Circle neighborhood of Charleston, South Carolina ninety-five paying guests had given a cumulative rating of 4.9 stars, making me a "Superhost." Its black and white gingham check pinch-pleated drapes I´d had custom-made to reference both the neighborhood's heritage as housing for the Old Navy Yard workers, and the Luxe black-lacquered Chinese chests. The Hollywood Regency pure brass faux bamboo etagere, which held vintage board games, a smart TV loaded with Netflix and premium cable TV, and the requisite Hummel and Scotty dog kitsch – all original.

New, old stock wall-paper in peach toile with tiny plants and wrought iron flower carts that I bought from same vendor who supplied the hit TV show *Madmen* complemented the bathroom's original 1960 peach fixtures. My towel bars were handmade by the Amish. The hospitality toiletries were locally-made, and organic. The refrigerator I kept stocked with organic yogurts, breads, fresh strawberries. I had a variety of coffees and teas. I equipped a library with local tour books, and classics of literature, and an adjustable drafting table, and high-speed internet. Outside in the sprawling yard under moss-draped Live Oak trees overlooking Noisette Creek I´d installed an old-fashioned oak swing, and a wooden picnic table. My bed linens and pillows were premium, some even made in America.

Two weeks before staying in my own guest house I'd been surrounded by the whispering trees, gurgling koi pond, and my own eclectic, curated art and clean furnishings in the Mount Pleasant home I'd lived in for 15 years. That seemed a lifetime ago, before I was solicited on a train, and met "my" Portuguese attorney, who urged me to sell it, promising he'd have my Portuguese visa waiting for me when I arrived. I still owned two Victorian apartments on Hampton Park. I rented them long-term to a national magazine art editor, a Brooklyn specialty food company founder, a city planner, and marketing director for an upscale resort community, herself owner of two guest cottages I've no doubt were also very nicely appointed. What I did not know then was that my attorney had arranged for me to pay equivalent of an annual Portuguese salary to live for six months in this dump.

Propped against a wall - as there was no piece of furniture I cared to sit on - my twenty-three years of training under the auspices of the scrupulous Charleston Trident Association of Realtors held me upright. I informed this company of swindlers that Black Mold is such a serious health hazard in the US that landlords and real estate agents who simply fail to disclose it may be prosecuted criminally, the afflicted buildings ordered torn down. The agents agreed to have the mold removed at 9 a.m. Monday morning. Emboldened I added I could not be held responsible for accidentally breaking the lady's *nice things* when trying to find a spot to set my computer, or a tea cup. After some wrangling between themselves they agreed to remove what I marked or set aside the following week.

My mind raced over all what had been done to me by people who I had every reason to trust as my legal fiduciaries. Only gradually a rising staccato chattering pierced my fog. The gist of their arguing was that the matron demanded the agents conveyed to me in the strongest possible terms that under *no circumstance* was I ever to open a window. In that event dust would enter, *ruining her valuable things.* The fact that it was already 37 degrees in July and the apartment had no air conditioning was no concern of hers. Stepping over the tangled cords from the lamp contest, I took one of the two, jailer-sized key rings I noticed, and began to shovel the three of them out my door. The explanations of which passcodes went with each key the silver fox agent began were in Portuguese, and would have been completely incomprehensible to me in any language, anyway. I was able to lock them all out well enough.

I staggered up the stairs, choosing the larger of the two bedrooms. Rummaging through the scarred bureaus that lined every wall upstairs I found a serviceable terrycloth bath towel. I ripped down the green plastic shower curtain from two decades earlier in what was a tomb-like, windowless bathroom lined in black granite, and discovering the bathtub had no drain plug, went back to the bureaus until I found a wash rag to stuff in the drain hole. I ran a bath, bathed, and took my summer nightgown out of one suitcase, and the thin, down pillow. I threw off the ancient foam pillows littering the bed onto the floor, and collapsed on my new bed.

I was still trying to get comfortable on the strangely hard, unpadded mattress early the next morning at seven a.m.- two a.m. early South Carolina time to be precise - when I became aware of men's voices shouting underneath my window. I put my thin pillow over my head and when that did no good, I felt around on the floor for the foam pillows, boxing my head in completely. But, no number or type of pillows could have muffled the noise that began next. It began with a roar. It became a continuous growl, and soon it was punctuated by brutal clanging of metal on metal. I opened my eyes, and with horror saw a yellow claw the size of a bathtub hovering a few feet from my window. It looked like a wrecking ball. I jumped up and looked out the window. There was no street in front of my building. There was no street in either direction. A giant gash ran up and down the street as far as I could see in either direction. This raw trench was partly filled with muddy water and bordered by mountains of russet dirt and broken clay pipe. On top of the gutted earth piles two-story tall earth-moving machines climbed. Across the trench through the rust-colored haze I saw small stores and 19th century townhouses all boarded up, all covered in thick, rust-colored dust.

The third thing I noticed about the apartment was that it was located directly on the city's long-term sewage pipe replacement project. The bright yellow, and orange machines—a detail I mention as they were the only bits of color in an otherwise lifeless and moribund area—roared to life five mornings a week at seven. On Saturdays they started at eight. Each day they stopped for one hour for lunch, then continued until seven or eight in the evening. With my back pressed against the back upstairs laundry porch wall - the furthest I could get away from the brouhaha - my cell phone Record Level stayed in the red Distortion Zone. The noise was deafening, and constant. A simple phone conversation was impossible. Shouting at the top of my lungs, repeating myself constantly, and hanging up as soon as possible with a splitting headache was what happened.

As far as I could tell no one else lived in the building which was thirty or forty apartments, except possibly one very young man, and the family of three that lived next to me. One day I shared a ride in the elevator with a shy older woman in sensible shoes, a domestic worker sent to dust her client's things in their now-uninhabitable, constantly dust-filling apartment. Another day I forgot the passcode to enter my building, and I slipped in behind the very young man in his aspirational business suit in another wing. I wandered the airless halls hearing only my footsteps, not seeing another living soul.

The family next door to me seemed fractured, and doing a remarkable job reassembling itself. The brother was tall, broodingly handsome with slim hips and wide shoulders of a swimmer. No older than 16, he already had the care-worn face of a middle-aged man. His little sister looked eight or nine. Their diminutive dark-haired mother I rarely saw. I heard her singing though in the evenings in dulcet tones of a bird from the small back balcony, or the small back bedroom that she shared with her daughter because our doors were always open. (I moved into the smaller bedroom, farther from the machines my second night.) Behind textured glass panels that separated our balconies I saw blurred leaves and blossoms of plants, green, pink and red. Their leaves tickled the edges of the glass. Sundays, and evenings the family returned from grocery shopping together. The little girl warbled happily, cheerful chirping drifting through our opened kitchen windows, our only source of ventilation on the front of the apartments, although they only opened to a glassed in hallway.

One day I stopped in front of the rear entrance to avoid being run over by a long, white Mercedes sedan that pulled rapidly out from the underground parking garage. It was driven by a scowling, jowly man with dramatic, wavy silver hair, who I judged to be French, or Spanish, maybe *from the Algarve,* and another investor in this building. If he was one of the original developers, I had no pity for him.

The complex was built in the panopticon prison style, a four-story horseshoe surrounding a central stone courtyard where inmates are observable at all times. There were no trees or shrubs or any object that could conceal a person, or provide shelter or shade from sun or rain, nor require maintenance. There was a tiny patch of grass like a goatee on a fat man's face in the center of the expanse of gray stone, and on this sat a child's basic, backyard playset; two swings and a slide. It appeared to be an afterthought to market the apartments to young families who might like the idea of their children being locked behind a two-story concrete wall requiring a complicated set of keys and passwords to enter, and being observable at all times from all windows. Twice I sat on the ledge waiting for the machines to stop, and watched two young couples with three small children near the play set. They never ventured far from each other, and they never stayed more than a few minutes, and I'm certain that they did not live there.

The two-bedroom units with their cell-sized bedrooms, "open floor plan" of a single common room, single-pane aluminium windows, and electric baseboard heating - cheapest to install and the most costly to operate, like trying to heat a house with electric toasters – their layers of security and their veneer of polished stone were surely sold as "luxury," in a "privileged area". This squandered mass of back-breakingly quarried stone and poured concrete was built in a low spot on a tight alley. Across from the apartment complex was a dinosaur carcass rising from a moat of stagnant water like

La Brea Tar Pits. Its concrete blocks rib cage was topped with rusted rebar resembling tufts of animal hair. Beyond this spectral specimen reaching upwards in supplication the vista terminated at a massive façade of unfinished concrete blocks on a rise catty-cornered across from my hotel. (The facade was demolished two years later.)

The whole area appeared to have been developed soon after Portugal joined the European Union in 1986 when loan money poured in. The area was like a monumental sculpture garden dedicated to hubris, like former sites of the international Olympics.

With no thought given to parking or to sidewalks, patrons of an optimistic twenty-four-hour veterinary clinic next to the dinosaur carcass park around the corner of the short alley, and walk their pets in the alley. In the center of the alley is a gurgling fountain. Some days it fills the alley. I try and shout to stop people from splashing through it, because this fountain is raw sewage. Some days five or six inches deep, during dry spells its edge becomes a friable, wind-born dust that mixes with the dust from the trench digging out front.

Like the sewage fountain, the key to the apartment is staying out of it. My first trip was to my attorney, where I was fired when I balked at his €3,800 bill itemized as "Golden Visa research," after he´d presented himself as a "Visa Expert," and with no visa process even begun. My next trip was to Century 21, where I was elegantly laughed at (very elegantly) all the way up to Century 21 Iberia headquarters, even after I showed its owners that their agent Paulo had expressly fabricated "concerning clauses" he said were in the lease of the apartment I found and wanted to rent, and which did not appear at all in that document.

With no other choice I could see, after wasting so much money and now assuming additional indefinite storage fees of $400 a month for my things back in the US, I settled into a routine of roaming, always on the move, always looking for something positive, something good, something beautiful, some kindness, some honesty, some wi-fi, or some air conditioning in the city I'd trusted to be my new home.

With my few changes of clothes becoming ragged, my savings as gouged as the street in front of my apartment, no idea when I might see my things again or when anything might improve, sleep-deprived, carrying the stench of the unloved, truly anyone who let me sit with them out of the heat for a few hours really was beautiful and kind.

It can take an hour to stretch my back after the short night of sweat-soaked tossing on the rock-hard mattress. Even the nights are not always quiet or peaceful here. I soon learn that my neighborhood is "privileged" primarily for its prostitutes, another of its pitfalls. Long after the machines have silenced for the day the stillness is frequently punctuated by loud negotiations under my window, and startled cries as drunks fall or are pushed into the open sewer pipe trench.

If I wake up with time to spare before the machines roar back to life, I make coffee by boiling water in an old Teflon/aluminium saucepan, catching its peeling flakes along with the coffee grounds in a sieve that I found in a drawer underneath a German calendar with its top page suggesting the last occupant of this apartment fled six months earlier, and was also an *estrangeiro*.

To conserve funds, I eat just one real meal a day, usually at the hotel's breakfast buffet where I fill up on fresh fruits and vegetables, bacon, sliced cheeses, fresh orange juice, baked beans, and stewed tomatoes and linger in the air conditioning, enjoying the view of the city afforded by the Brutalist tower, and pretending that I am also just a normal, happy tourist.

Sometimes I speak to other people in English. My orange backpack with my laptop computer, its clunky accessories, and 1.5-liter water bottle, is always by my side as going back to the apartment is impossible with the noise until the machines stop briefly for lunch.

From there I sometimes head to the boxes on the doorstep of an abandoned nineteenth-century townhouse that serves as this neighborhood's grocery store to rummage a couple of carrots or pieces of fruit. Then I settle my pack on my back, and wander the city until after 7 p.m. Photos taken of me at this time show me chiselled, firm, with muscled legs, and tautly-defined cheekbones.

Other than a very few basic coffee shops struggling to stay open with little to sell but coffee, packaged drinks and squashed-looking, mass-produced pastries there is little to see in this immediate area. One Sunday fragments of pottery caught my eye at the side of the pit. I picked them up one by one, washed them and displayed them on my kitchen window sill, imagining them coughed up by the ghosts of Rome. I told myself over time I would surely uncover their stories, and piece together a new life for myself here somehow.

Several days I came upon the Very Tall Man who sits or stands perfectly still in the dusty pocket park behind the recycling bins. He stands like an egret, never speaking. He has no basket for coins. He wears a different, beautifully tailored three-piece suit in a different dream-like color each time I see him. His skin is almost blue-black and his suits are luscious electric blue, magnificent magenta, deep lavender, or off-white with a hint of cream, always spotless, always with a top hat, waistcoat, jacket, trousers, and a crisp, white dress shirt. He presents himself as a jewel at the end of the open sewer pipe trench, where almost no one is ever nearby to notice him. This is how I know I am in the presence of a great artist.

The man chasing the pig did not want to be noticed, or at least not noticed being dragged by a pig. Three blocks up the hill from the apartment where the street begins again, I found a small park blessed by two shade trees, and even a bench. I was sitting, swilling water one hot August day and looked around. Across the street an abandoned yellow Art Deco building with a curved corner was covered in spires of Arabic-inspired graffiti. A few doors down, was a dusty store displaying hot water boilers. I swivelled around just in time to see a door open in a nondescript, light-colored apartment building, and a pig bolt out. The pig was a huge, black and white "pot-bellied" pig briefly fashionable in the US as a pet. (Did this fad end when the BBQ and bacon-ice cream fads began?) A long rope followed the pig, and at the end was a thin man in a white guayabera shirt and light-colored pants, smoking a cigarette. The man looked like a cigarette. He was cool and lean, and all legs, while the pig was all stomach, and in a hot trot.

They were roughly the same size, but their weights were distributed differently.

The pig ran dragging the man, and the man leaned back trying to maintain an effortless saunter as he smoked his cigarette creating a curious "saunter-run," the first and only such method of locomotion I've ever seen. Twice they were almost hit by oncoming cars before disappearing around the corner near the boiler shop. I hiked back this way several times hoping to see them again. I asked around at the nearby coffee shops if anyone knew anything about them. I asked a woman walking her Shih Tzu outside her Antas apartment farther up the hill, where the city became more civilized. We had a very pleasant conversation. She was new to the area, too. But no one I spoke to knew anything about the man or the pig, or had ever seen them.

Monday morning, I fled the apartment for the hotel breakfast before seven, returning at nine to let in the "Black Mold Remediation Team;" two small, elderly painters. I left them alone with the ear-splitting machines trolling inches from them, with some guilt, but this was brute survival. The men returned the following day, and the following week to remove the detritus I'd set aside. All the Post-it Note pads I'd packed in the US really came in handy. I also filled six plastic shopping bags with plastic shopping bags, and used plastic restaurant carry-out containers that were jammed into the kitchen cabinets and pantry, and two more full-sized plastic trash bags and several smaller bags with coat hangers so tightly packed in the built-in wardrobes upstairs that they sprang out like giant, broken Slinky toys, with sharp, poking metal edges when I tried to pry out just a few at a time.

The men took away the bags, and a few boxes of china and bric-a-brac that I could not fit into any cupboard or drawer, but they refused to take away the dried blood colored sofa bed, although its metal rods were so thoroughly worked up through the stuffing that layers of folded blankets I'd initially laid on for hygiene and kept adding to, did nothing to cushion the bars enough to make it comfortable to sit on. They refused to take away the legless foam sofa, which threw me to the floor on top of its clattering chrome "arm" the first time I sat on it. The two gentlemen even refused to take away the brown vinyl recliner with its commanding view of the sewer trench, and its arms covered in cigarette burns and ink. Soon enough though I was able to share all of this, and somehow more with someone who really appreciated it.

It was another Thursday night at about 10 p.m. I was waiting for the final exhaustion to settle in before trudging home to the apartment, slumped in my usual spot at the edge of the burgundy banquette. My computer was open on the bar table Sérgio had carried across from his area. The boiled-onion gaze of James Dean considered the cleavage of Jessica Lange in *King Kong*'s grip across his 1957 Chevy hood. The Thursday night vocalist had finished her caterwauling. The guitar player had finished his beer with Sérgio, and disappeared into the city, and my complimentary glass of delicious dinner wine was long gone. The doors to the lobby kept opening and closing an unusual amount for this time of night. I glanced over to see a knot of people collecting in the small area between the doors and the check-in counter. I counted almost fifty in all. They were packed four deep. These new arrivals all had a stunned look, like people who had been through something horrible together.

Rita, the manager was working late that night. She came to my alcove leading a large man with a bear-like appearance. They stood in front of me. The man's shoulders sagged, and he gave off a rank, animal odor. Rita spoke to the man quietly, and as if trying to calm a small child. I was not trying to eavesdrop on their conversation, but they were basically talking in my lap. The tower hotel lobby was so compact on each floor, and by now I was such a fixture I must have blended in as just another of the oddball, old, American characters like those in the mural behind me.

Rita was trying various languages. I picked up words in Portuguese, English, and French. The man stared at Rita uncomprehendingly. It turned out he did not understand any of those languages, but I did, and I understood that Rita was telling the man there was no room for him in the inn. Rita was trying to also explain that she had called every other hotel in the city she knew of, and none had an available room except one twenty-three kilometers away.

The man's face was turning a purplish color, as if he was strangling. His pale eyes were watering. His sweating became uncontrollable. I spoke up. They seemed to notice me sitting a few feet away from them for the first time, although I was no more than four feet from them. Rita told me the man was the tour bus driver. He had delivered this large group to Portugal from Bulgaria, and in return his employer had sold his room out from under him for a last-minute paying guest. I made the instant calculation writer Malcom Gladwell devoted his book, *Blink* to: if this man had been in charge of driving 50 people across Europe, he was probably a decent fellow. I told Rita that I might have a solution. As squalid as my apartment was, it had an extra room with a private bath. It was located just behind the hotel. I said the man was welcome to stay there for a few nights. I did not want any money. Rita somehow explained my offer to the man, and vouched for us both. The tour company was a regular client of her hotel. I'd been there almost every day and night for over a month.

The man looked at me with such gratitude as I have only seen before or since on the faces of small children and dogs. He went to get his things as I packed away my laptop, returning with a small, cloth carry-on bag, and a large, dark backpack. He went back to have a few words with his tour group, who I saw now were all sunburned and shivering like leaves in the air-conditioning blast. The group all turned to look me over with neither alarm nor admiration that I could discern. Together the man and I left the hotel walking side by side, backpack by backpack.

We crossed the broken granite courtyard, and entered into the dark alley at the side of the hotel. It opened and we passed the public housing project, with its racks of iron conduit pipe for communal drying of laundry now vacant. As tired as I was from my days on the move, poor sleep, sketchy nutrition, the man was in much worse shape. He was so exhausted that each individual step he took seemed to be a miracle. I worried constantly that he would collapse. Given his large size, even unencumbered I never would have been able to help him up. So, I kept up an encouraging patter,

"Just around the corner. Just a little farther. Just a little more," I said smiling. My smile was genuine. I was truly happy and excited to have my first house guest in my new home country.

We stepped around the gurgling sewage fountain. For once I remembered the gate passcode and key combination on the first try. We climbed the steps into the courtyard, whereupon seeing I really had taken him to an apartment complex, the man seemed to revive a little. I remembered even the passcode to the outside building door, and to the elevator, for once not needing to check the slip of paper with the code that I kept folded in my wallet. After a pungent elevator ride under the harsh glare of florescent light, I opened the apartment door. The man gazed around him in wonder as if entering a truly splendid place. It did look better. The black mold had been freshly painted over. The garbage bags, and Post It Note pile removals had made a noticeable difference, although only seeing it through his eyes did I realize this.

I showed the man to the master bedroom, explaining about the machines beginning promptly at seven. I conveyed this information with theatrical miming, and words in various languages. I used the fingers of my hand to inform him of the hour at which his ears would pour forth blood. I demonstrated ears bleeding, or exploding. This was no problem at all for the man, who had to be at the hotel very early every morning to breakfast with his group, and sort out any issues before beginning the day's tour began.

There was one nice thing about the apartment, which now I enjoyed. It had a generous supply of very fine bed linens. They packed every drawer in every scarred bureau and wardrobe so tightly that I had to leave my things in my suitcases. But on this night I took pleasure selecting just the right things for my visitor.

There were cotton percales worn to silk-like smoothness, and hand-embroidered, and crochet-edged sheets and pillowcases of real linen. There were plenty of bath towels. The man appeared purple in part, because he was sunburned. Because he was also distraught, I chose a cool, smooth peach percale in a soothing, faded, floral of tea roses from the 1970s, and a matching set of oversized terrycloth towels in a masculine tan color. We made up his bed together. I brought soap to his bathroom, gave him one of the jailer-sized sets of keys, and bid him good night. Downstairs I wrote on a series of Post-It Notes all the passcodes I'd worked out through trial and error, pasting them on the front door, where he'd see them in the morning when he left.

We saw each other only once more over the three nights that he stayed. He was gone most morning before I got up, but I heard him from behind his closed door when I returned in the evenings, speaking and laughing softly with his family. Through a combination of French, English, Portuguese, German, and Bulgarian I learned that he had been on the road working back-to-back tours for the bus company for almost three months with no vacation and had not seen his wife or his two children in all that time. His son was seven, and his daughter was nine. He had been at the airport ready to finally board a flight home to Sofia, Bulgaria when the call came from his boss. The ultimatum was either return to work this two-week tour of Portugal, or become jobless.

Each day we sent each other polite, little roommate texts, "Be back at 8." "Bom dia. Obrigado." I never really understood his name. I think it was *Hristo*, which I pronounced *Cristo*, like the performance artist who draped sheets over cities. After three nights, I came home to this:

Thank You VeRY, VERY VERY MUCh!

YOU ARE EVERY TIME WELCOME IN BULGARIA

You are every time welcome in Bulgaria.

Sofia 1000

Malyovica – Str 2

Cristo

It was written on a folded A-4 sheet of paper that I recognized from the hotel´s printouts of immigration documents and housing listings for me. It was written in not exactly what you could call calligraphy, but something akin. Each letter was very carefully drawn with the spaces between the letters measured out equally. The exclamation point at the end of the first line was an open triangle with a circle below it. It all looked full of joy. It was as full of joy as anything I have ever seen made with a ballpoint pen.

My first three weeks in that apartment I suffered violent food poisoning twice before realizing the refrigerator "set" only to the correct temperature for incubating pathogens. (It later quit altogether). I was propositioned six times by taxi drivers, who based on my location, and probably assuming I was still in my forties, but worn down by my profession assumed I was a prostitute. One night the electricity went out with an explosion, showering me with dozens of tiny, glass shards when I flipped on the overhead light switch after a long day on the streets.

I lasted seven weeks in that apartment. Thanks to Rita and Sérgio, and the other hotel staff who kept me alive, treated me with dignity, helped me find a house to buy, and helped me apply for a Portuguese bank loan, I was able to find and buy an affordable house. In the interim before my loan closed and the seller was ready to move, that real estate agent had arranged another apartment for me to rent. It was also an inflated price, and its French landlady lived downstairs. She had a habit of entering my apartment whenever I left to rearrange my things. One day she moved my shoes out of the bedroom closet, and I eventually found them in a Chinese chest near the front door. She went through and reorganized all of my papers. Another day I found a pair of her used acetate underpants on the chest, and my linen sundress missing. It was pale duck egg with brown and cream palm trees from my former home in *The Palmetto State*. But, that apartment was clean, and nicely furnished for an occasionally visiting son. It had a working kitchen, new coffee machine, refrigerator, TV, internet, even art and a piano. There was a print shop right across the street, a real grocery store two blocks down. The beach was within walking distance, and there was no bulldozer, no prostitute, and no sewage fountain in sight.

The seven weeks I lasted at the first apartment had cost me nearly €12,000, including my attorney's "Golden Visa Research," fees but, it was priceless to a Bulgarian bus driver. It was so priceless that he gave me all of Bulgaria in return.

Hello, Dog!

A neighbor is carefully massaging a knit top before she hangs it on her short clothes line sagging four-stories up in a six-story building of concrete painted mustard and brown.

My house sits behind a two-story wall of concrete that divides the apartments from the houses. The houses are mostly three-and four-story, attached on one side, exclusively made of concrete. This is very funny to me because the people who own them all seem to have made their money in the selling of soft things.

HELLO, DOG!

Two of my immediate neighbors own bakeries. Another retired as the manager of a German-owned leather goods factory. My basement includes a walk-in cooler built by the original owners to hold soft cheeses they distributed for Nestlé.

The two-story concrete wall conceals a green commons that snakes between our houses and the apartments like the Rio Grande River that separates Americans from Mexicans. It is a no-go zone here for other reasons I´ll explain later.

The man-made canyon walls seem to create odd air currents that attract birds. Seagulls sail like white pillowcases over a smoothed bed, although we are five kilometers from the sea. Pigeons soar below the seagulls pretending to be graceful swallows. The actual swallows are mousy, brown little *passeiros* that spend their days in hiding under the leaf cover. Twice each day I hear them, though. In the cool mornings at 5:45 they wake me to sing outside my window in the red and green *photinia* between my driveway and Nina's. There must be fifty or sixty of them at least, but when I lift my head and look blearily out, all I ever see are the trembling leaves. They sing exactly ten minutes, then are silent, resuming a longer concert at the dimming of each day.

As the day progresses, I'm awoken again by the curious receding calls of seagulls - with their false bonhomie. At midday a Eurasian Collared Dove calls. I had assumed this was a particularly soulful pigeon, or even the designated singer of the flock like a Jewish cantor, but no. Lemon Spooner, (a real person, a Portuguese wildlife enthusiast) sets me straight, "They sound similar. The pigeons are iridescent green and grey. The doves here are often a white domestic variety, or the wild, collared dove, which is a soft pinky- grey." I imagine black, Eurasian headphones slung 'round the back of her pinky-grey neck as the unseen dove sings, *How can you just leave me standing, alone in a world that's so cold?*

HELLO, DOG!

The pigeons and seagulls are swooping toward the neighbor's clean laundry now. Nina barks. She growls menacingly. Nina is a Border Collie, the breed of strategic thinkers that herds large groups of animals much larger than themselves, then cocks their heads and asks, *Is that all you got?* Nina cannot see the laundry or the green commons. Nina sees only the patch of sky directly above her walled concrete enclosure, but she knows the birds are up to no good. I climb up the stairs to my garage roof, the place that Nina and I can see each other fully. I tell her that I admire her dedication, but *Those birds will poop and pee where they please. They are not like us* I say.

The apartment of my neighbor is part of a set of apartments between two other sets, like three years of encyclopedias from the 1970s; one Celery Green, one Mustard and Brown, and her set, Harvest Gold. They line the commons with more sets, separating it from a thoroughfare once a major artery linking Porto's northern inland towns of Senhora da Hora, Custóias, São

Mamede de Infesta, Leça de Ballio, and Rio Tinto with the industrial beach town of Matosinhos; motto: "World's Best Seafood."

Matosinhos once had many fish canneries, and a penicillin factory, which brought my friend, Bette from Denmark in the Seventies with her husband, who came to manage it. The town has an oil refinery, though it will soon be moved. My town, Senhora da Hora was home to the sprawling Efanor textile factory from 1902 to 1992. At the height of its operations the factory employed 3,000 workers. Its brick smokestack still stands. The thoroughfare brought people from all over northern Portugal to the 200-shop *Centro Comercial Londres*, which is at the end of my street. That building reaches seventeen stories, all made of concrete. Built in 1982 it was the largest commercial center in northern Portugal throughout 1980s and 1990s. When the factory closed in 1992 the land was redeveloped to make the country's largest shopping mall. The newer, *Estrada da Circunvalação* thoroughfare was built to fling cars into the new shopping malls that began to change the traditional shopping experience, which was pedestrian and neighborly.

The old thoroughfare, *Rua Nova de São Gens* now sees mainly local traffic. After the big three sets of apartment buildings the road is lined with newer, six- and eight-plex apartment buildings, and diminutive, pre-war social housing of unpainted concrete. There are also still pocket-sized pet food shops, a used bicycle shop, dusty coffee shops indistinguishable from each other under concrete awnings, bus stops with benches, and others just metal poles, a corner hardware store painted vivid green, (of course, concrete), two two-bay auto repair shops, a scattering of cheerful, little *papelarias*, a few exhausted, old boarded up manor houses weeping tears of cement through blindfolds of hollow orange block. But in a two-mile stretch there is not a single tree. With its green commons, the small pocket park across from my house, staggered roofline streetscape, and tiny front yards behind fences my neighborhood is very popular with dogs.

There must be more than two hundred dogs living in this dense three blocks. I know only a few notables. Nina is black and white. To my left is a tan German Shepherd that I have only seen once by standing on tiptoes on my upper balcony and looking down into what looked like a dry, concrete well. Skipping over a house with a large, extended family of mixed-race cats, is the distinctive Bruno, a gargoyle-like Rottweiler. Directly across from me Max, the lucky little Jack Russell lives with António, Conceição and Elsa. Max has free run of grass front and side, and he gets two walks a day. But, most of the dogs here live behind walls or fences of solid steel or concrete, with concrete beneath their feet, or inside in the concrete apartments.

Max´s neighbors to the left are two large dogs I know only from snouts visible through slits in the steel gate. Around the corner a pony-sized, grey Mastiff lives. He lopes by with his owner, a boyish, middle-aged man in loose, faded jeans, the two of them like a couple of slim-hipped cowboys. A magnificent, coal-black German Shepherd appears in the park from time to time leading a denim-clad young man who wears sunglasses in all weather. Then, there is the diminutive, black French Papillon spaniel with a white chest and dramatic white ear tufts. She picks her way daintily through the park grass attached to an old man who wears that flat-wedge, colorless cap that old men wear everywhere in the Western World.

A pure white Dandie Dinmont terrier strides before her ectomorph, dressed always in a black, two-piece, American-labelled tracksuit, always preoccupied with his cell phone. One of those pale, pointed dogs that look to me like sugar cookies stamped out, and baked by the dozens rides in with a woman who manages to look like both her dog, and her red Mini Cooper; pale, thin, wearing white and red. They go into the park, do their business efficiently, and get back in, and drive away. Retired French teachers, António and Alcina have two dogs. I don´t know them well; one is a grey terrier. The other is white and short-haired. The new owners next door to them have twin babies, (human) and two large dogs kept behind a new, solid steel and concrete fence.

The jovial white Labrador pads down the hill, his sight-impaired young owner click-clacketing her white cane on the sidewalk. The German Shepherd - intensely frightening because he is behind one of the few open fences on the street - has moved. The new owners have a Beagle. Malu - short for Maria Luísa – is a medium-sized white poodle of indeterminate confirmation, legendary for slipping her leash. Her owner, Melania then wanders the neighborhood calling, *Malu, Malu! Malu, Malu!* her normally pleasant voice shrill with anxiety. I worry too. I wonder if Malu is smart about cars. The thoroughfare is near. (Malu always comes back).

HELLO, DOG!

The woefully overweight Labrador waddles behind his well-shod gentleman who wears thick, rubber-soled shoes. (Dogs don't have the footwear for this place). I am outside one day in my yard directly in front, when this Labrador, and the obese French Bulldog with the woman I think looks a little like me on a bad day prepare a clumsy attack. The woman bends to pick up her dog. Her glasses slide down her nose and her loose ponytail gets snarled in her dog's bared teeth. Unsocialized dogs don't know how to behave in public, and I'm crabby too when my feet hurt.

Rottweilers protected Roman cattle merchants when they crossed the Alps. The dogs carried the money around their necks in pouches. How a Rottweiler wound up on a small balcony is something Bruno must ask himself every day. Some days Bruno is allowed into the side yard that borders the path that links the apartments and *Rua de São Gens* with the houses and pocket park. Bruno's fence is open post. It is on the inside curve of a concrete wall on the convex, and the path is one meter wide. So, at most pedestrians are one meter from Bruno's barking, big, lunging head, but more often they are taken by complete surprise from a distance of twelve inches.

I have tried reasoning with this dog in both *inglês* and *portuguese*. I've called him *Sweet Pea* and *minha vizinho* (my neighbor). I've tried shame: *Oh, for Heaven's sake! I am your neighbor! I live three houses down!* I've tried eye contact, (which is terrifying because there is madness in Bruno's eyes) and I've tried dismissively withholding eye contact. Bruno takes work seriously. After three years Bruno has eased up, now lunging and barking once or twice to show that he is not shirking on the job, while simultaneously wagging his tail. The Portuguese say, *A barking dog does not bite.* This is about Portuguese people, not dogs. I wish I could be certain that Bruno would not rip my arm off if I tried to pet him through the bars.

HELLO, DOG!

It's best we keep our relationship professional. I thank him briskly for his service, and move on.

Recently for the very first time that I walked by him, Bruno did not bark, but looked at me dolefully, as if regretting that the rigors of his breeding had forced him to behave so harshly toward me. I also may have underestimated his intellect based on his limited vocal range compared to Nina's. He never once barked I realized at the blind woman and her Labrador.

Bruno has just two barks: a seal-like *Arf! Arf!* and the hearty deep *Bow-wow* that one expects of a Rottweiler. Nina can do both of those. Nina can also imitate the alto, and the light baritone of the two dogs across from her, who I know only by their snouts in the fence slits. She *yips* like lucky, little Max. She plays with a deep throat growling like Himalayan throat singing, (but to her may be an ancestral channelling of wolf belching bone fragments of prey). Nina does a soft warbling, a self-comforting yodel, and a sharp call to action.

But her specialty is keening—a wail, which really gets the other dogs going. Together the unseen dogs sound like a siren. Most have never seen each other. Many have never seen another human other than glimpses of those who live next door to them, but Nina has knit them together into a community of sounds.

I met Nina only once. Her steel gate was open when I was walking back from the recycling bins at the commercial center, carrying an empty pail. Nina was halfway down her driveway. She saw me, took a few steps forward, then froze, a foot poised mid-air. Her owner, Paulo´s ugly snarl began. *Nina!* This is the only way I have ever heard him acknowledge her at all, with reproach and disgust. His live-in girlfriend's eight-year-old daughter mimics this snarl perfectly to please her mother´s patron. Fearing an electric shock collar I froze. Suddenly, Nina ran. I dropped the empty pail. Nina leapt up, putting her stiff outstretched legs on my shoulders as if holding me in a full-body hug, and I patted her as one does a distressed child, using both hands both to steady myself against her, and as she is very large. Nina has a human face. Her eyes are greenish-yellow-gold, like honey made from linden flowers. Paulo grabbed her collar, still screaming at her, though I told him I did not mind at all, that I loved her. Nina held her eye contact with me the whole time, although I swear, she winked at me, *Don't worry. I can handle this bully.* But the thing is; I don't think she can.

Since that day we've only seen fragments of each other through bare patches in the *photinia*. I singsong whenever I go out and come in, *Nina, Nina, Nina* to let her know that I know she is still in there. Some days I hear her scrabbling an empty plastic flower pot across her patch of concrete.

When I first saw this house I was desperate to move from an apartment in a vacant building in a section of Porto favored by prostitutes. Worse, the building had been vacated, along with every other building for three blocks, because the street had been completely excavated for a massive sewer replacement project. This was something that my attorney whose office was seven minutes away would have known. This member in good standing with the Ordem dos Advogados was nameed *Coelho,* (rabbit) but he was a chicken-chested little weasel, who had obligated me to pay six months´ rent in advance, directing where to wire the money while I was still in the United States. The two times I met him, he busied himself inspecting his dark blue suit for lint specks, flicking them off whenever I spoke. Six days a week giant earth-moving and pipe-busting machines roared, clanked, and spewed acrid dust. The apartment had no air conditioning, no internet, no functioning refrigerator, and was filled with cast-off, broken, decades-old furnishings, including the concrete-hard mattress.

I bought the first house I saw. It had a paved street in front. The owner's eight-year-old grandson led me on his private tour, weaving between an overgrown, dense jungle of azaleas, camelias, and rubbery Bird-of-Paradise shrubs where I imagined yellow, spotted leopards lounging in the dense shade. He showed me hiding spaces underneath the outside stairs near a lemon tree, and on the third-floor landing inside, where a small window was a secret peep hole out. I wrote a Promissory Note on a scrap of paper, and made his father take me to the bank immediately, where I gave him €1,000 as earnest money.

If the front yard was a painting by the artist, Rousseau, the back yard was strictly Edward Gorey, or even, Grady Gordon. The back yard terrified me. Everything was concrete, or a tile made to look like concrete. High, lumpy, concrete walls veined in black mold conjured a tableau of emaciated Nazi death camp inmates writing in agony. There was a shoulder-wide drain in the center of the concrete driveway covered with a rusted metal trap door that I refused to acknowledge.

Once inside the home I was able to see over that wall to a lush, green commons stretching on. I imagined neighborhood picnics, festivals, fathers flying kites on Sundays. I thought of maybe donating a bench, and a few trees and getting involved in organizing mural painting on the walls facing the commons. Nothing like this ever happened. In three years I saw only a handful of people in the commons. All except one couple pushing a baby carriage through then tall grass, who wished they hadn´t taken this short-cut, are attached in some way to dogs. Most of the people sit or stand on a low concrete wall bordering the path (Bruno´s path.) They talk on their phones, they noodle broken glass with their toes while the dogs get on with their business.

I turned my attentions to the front. Behind my rusting, black sheet-metal fence were a mature petal-pink azalea, a family of bitter, flowerless dwarf azaleas breaking their concrete planter-wall, a stunted white camelia stuffed in barely a foot of earth between yellowish sidewalk, metal fence, and low concrete retaining wall, an uncut, spindly jacaranda like Babar's *Madame* supported on a spiral iron cane, her boughs grown vertical in a grasp for sunlight then erupting above the underbrush in girlish purple curls, another gardenia I think was legitimately a dwarf variety, three, fat Bird of Paradise, a good-sized, double trunk, elephant-grey tree; both trunks chopped off head high, and in the center, two red camellia trees; giant, cherry lollypops reaching the third-story of the house, all of this in an area the size of two queen-sized mattresses.

One day I ventured beyond the neighborhood crossing *Rua Nova de São Gens* by foot. I came to an old concrete building painted stylized vines, with real plants arranged outside. Inside a cluttered shop was jammed with miniature bonsais, orchids and lots of things made out of tree bark. There were plants that looked like strands and strands of tiny blue-green pearls, and tall, spiky plants. No one was around, but two shaggy mountain dogs rushed out at me from a side room. I walked farther back in, and found myself in a sort of greenhouse/vintage furniture store, although nothing had a price tag. Beyond this I saw a semi-feral plant nursery. A giant man with shaggy, brown hair, an absent-minded air behind Coke-bottle-thick eyeglasses, and a restless, kinetic energy sometime later followed the dogs.

Normally, I buy a few seconds of time with my overly-theatrical charades - enough time say to get the attention needed to order a coffee. Ricardo is a patient person who stayed long enough to understand that I had a large, overgrown garden nearby in desperate need of help. (I may have mimed plants coming out of the ground to strangle me.) Amazingly, I was able to say the name of the street I lived on sufficiently to be understood and to describe the house. Ricardo knew it because his father had planted those trees for the former owner. Two weeks later Ricardo and his father – a trim, erect, equally strapping man with steely eyes and no glasses – showed up with a flatbed truck and three eager young men with shovels. As I ferried glasses of water flavored with lemons from my crooked tree leaning out over the driveway from a tiny pocket of earth, miraculously bearing literally hundreds of lemons – I alternated encouragement with shouts of, *Don't kill it,* as the men dug up the front yard. Ricardo donated half a dozen giant black rubber tree pots with handles he found lying around the back of his father's nursery, and he and his men dragged them filled with the transplanted shrubs to the flat roof of the garage and the BBQ kitchen. All of these houses have backyard BBQ houses that swallow up natural earth. I'd considered knocking mine down to plant grass, but it was too big an operation for a very limited gain of additional green.

I bought six bamboo trees, each about seven feet tall, and we hauled them up together. One day I went to Leroy Merlin to buy wooden trellis panels to cover those unspeakable black-veined walls. On discovering the French chain store wanted two weeks and almost more than I paid for the panels to deliver them, I dragged them outside, and waited until I saw two unsuspecting workers in a panelled truck in the parking lot. I lured them to take me home with them for a few extra euros on their lunch break. I barely needed to speak. I just struggled under the 4 X 6 foot panels, and held out my thumb in hitchhiking mode. The commercial center at the end of my street was known by the drivers, so all I needed to say was an occasional *direita,* and *esquerda.*

In all Ricardo spent a year working on the garden with me. We added oversized troughs of creeping blue rosemary, and cascading, lacey, lime green asparagus fern, passionfruit, kiwi, and some delicate, baby-pink flowering vine Ricardo insisted on. (I was happy just with green). These we draped and led over roof edges, and up the trellis´ to cover all traces of Auschwitz. Now, the apartment neighbors had one more patch of green to gaze down on, and a relocated magenta azalea, a white gardenia, and two orange-flowering Bird of Paradise, too.

Splurging, we moved back to the front yard. We brought *Madame* two young suitors; an erect variegated snake plant nearly her height found leaning against the stone wall in Ricardo´s father´s nursery where it eluded removal for decades, and a broad-shouldered, squat limoncello-colored tropical. We planted one on each side of her. Ricardo also sent a man who ripped off the rusting black sheet metal inch by inch, straining in a stained sleeveless white undershirt until he'd revealed the wrought-iron filigree underneath, with its delightful heart motif. Another of Ricardo's colleagues, a shy, expert welder, took away the gates, returning them with new bottom steel panels and I convinced the boss of two Brazilian men I met working down the street to loan me his workers to strip and repaint the fence. This operation taught me valuable lessons: Once I´d paid the boss enough to cover his payroll, he wouldn't let his men return to finish the work. After much rehearsing, and listening to online translations, I stormed down the street to where the boss lived, and stood shaking in his driveway demanding in portuguese, *meu dinheiro ou seu trabalho, amanhã!* in front of his concrete, electrical and plumbing subcontractors, and the two underpaid Brazilian employees louder and louder, ignoring his threats to call the police, until he agreed to send back his workers.

They painted the filigree the calming turquoise green of shallow seas. And, I´m proud to say children now hold tantrums here. Clamping tiny fists around the open bars, they resist being stuffed into their parent's cars. *Madame* and her suitors lend moral support. Young men sit in their cars parked out front listening to music. I now can see the parade of dogs and human neighbors passing by. Alberto walks by several times each day on his way to and from the *pastelaria* in the commercial center. He always turns and looks at my garden. If he sees me, he flashes his magnificent smile, lifting his lush, snowy-white moustache. He gives me a double thumbs-up, and shouts, *"Tudo bem?" Sim!* I bark back. (Alberto's dog, by the way, is a Boxer.) I get to admire Alberto's very stylish outfits; coordinated fair-isle sweater vests, long-sleeve dress shirts, and wide-wale, corduroy trousers. He has several complete outfits.

Behind me live two retired ladies I know. Melania is lithe and beautiful with silky, white shoulder-length hair. I've introduced you already to her poodle, Malu. Ernestina is short and boxy with wiry, short, salt-and-pepper hair, and the sweetest, most genuine smile. Each has pointed out her apartment's rear windows to me.

Sometimes we catch each other's eyes across the commons, and wave. Ernestina and Melania often meet in front of my garden. Then they lean over the fence to discuss its history, and plant biology, something I know nothing about in any language, except that dirt, water, and sun are involved. I just nod. Isabel is in the yellow house a few doors down. She is involved in dog rescue, and stops now and then to try and interest me in one of her latest rescues. Next to her is tiny Conceição. Like me, she has no car so we run into each other often walking around town. She has subtle auburn hair and wears a faux fox, fur-trimmed capelet. She stops me whenever we meet, alternately to scold me for not speaking Portuguese, or to sweep me into a sudden, passionate embrace. I can never tell which is coming. I think she thinks of me as trainable puppy, but, as one of the few people in the neighborhood without a pet of my own I'm more of a spinster aunt to all the animals here.

Quite a few of the animals who come through my fence are young or beaten-down-by-life birds seeking respite from the brutal local pecking order. They waddle forward expectantly on my stoop when I open the door, as if waiting their turn to be seen by the doctor. I give them water, and whatever food I have that I think they might eat, sunflower seeds, or oats, but never touch them or let them inside. They found a quiet sheltered place. Once one of the pigeons tried to get in from the opened, upper balcony doors. They walk sideways like sneaks. I saw it in time to shut the doors.

Once I went to wash dishes after friends with young children who run in and outside had the doors open, and I found an inch-and-a-half-long *passeiro* sitting at my kitchen sink. It was brown and blended in with the woodwork. I think he was one of the choral performers who got thirsty and just came in for a drink. He explored the cool interior at his leisure for a few hours, then flew back out. I´d have him back anytime. He left no mess.

Several times a day a pair of half-breed Siamese siblings from the house with too many cats between Bruno and the silent shepherd next door slip between the open fence pickets seeking affection and food. The black and white cat with the low-hanging belly stops in and the siblings slink away. This is really the yard of the black and white cat with the low-hanging belly. She whiles away hours luxuriating in the new sunbeams Ricardo opened space for, flipping back and forth, or she lies on the smooth stone steps leading up to a set of French doors, or she snoozes in the cool weeds beneath the giant, magenta azalea we moved up to the back roof. But, when I come outside her yellow eyes open wide. She flies down the driveway, up the stairs, leaps six feet up to the top of the wall ledge, and drops down two stories into the commons. I don´t know how she does it. She doesn´t look fit. One of these days she's not going to make it, so I postpone errands whenever I see her resting out in my garden.

One night I was lying on the sofa against the French doors reading *Rolling Stone*. The black and white cat came up behind me and gave one, two blood-curdling screams. I saw her from the corner of my eye. I did not get up. It was a miserable cold, rainy night, and my only other excuse is that I was reading Matt Taibbi. The one and only time she had ever asked me for anything, and I ignored her. This decision was to haunt me for months with images of drowning kittens until she returned, slimmer, grudgingly forgiving, which I know as she now comes less often to my garden.

One day a snail the size of a gigantic walnut appeared suddenly on the crown molding against the ceiling of an inside room with no outside door, or operable window. Snails are not speedy creatures, to race in through an open door like the *passeiro*. Their shells do not collapse to squeeze through cracks. For nine hours I did nothing but come into the room now and then to gawk in silent reverence. Who was this snail? How had she found the time to climb all that way up a white wall undetected, and, why? Finally, I pried her off. I could not concentrate on anything else. I carried her outside on a *Mad* magazine, not the latest issue, and sat her down under the limoncello tropical. I thought this was for her own good. There was no food or water in my house. But, had I ruined her plans to live somewhere exotic just once before she died when I put her back on that crummy earth? Is this how people who have been freed from an agrarian life of labor feel as they are paving over every bit of living earth?

After living here a few years I've decided that concrete calcifies the human heart, making it indifferent to the suffering of others. I learned early on to brace myself when entering a Porto city taxi cab. Drivers careened around blind curves in ancient, narrow lanes, and when they encountered pedestrians – often elderly people clutching heavy bags of fruit or potatoes, some already stumbling on the cobblestones, using canes - these drivers do not slow down, they speed up! I´ve seen it a million times! They clench their steering wheels tighter, stomping the gas pedal, bearing down, almost as if screaming, *Old man! Old woman? Your bones are tired from eighty years humping the lumpy granite and concrete? Walk faster! My life is hard, too!*

At this time, I always asked drivers, and everyone I met where they lived, as I was frantically looking for another place to live. Every taxi driver I queried lived in a concrete apartment. So did the attorney who signed my apartment lease, so did the three Century 21 real estate agents. Now that I use ride shares, many of the drivers are displaced white-collar workers who still live in houses with trees and grass around them. I can finally relax, and enjoy the rides instead of rehearsing my role in impending homicides.

Dogs are social-justice advocates. One could do a lot worse than following their lead on many social issues. Portuguese dogs have also been helpful to me in developing my Portuguese language skills. I've found the queuing system here is a very good idea. Paper tickets are released from a machine, each customer takes a number then waits in line until their number is shown on a screen. This system is everywhere; deli counters, post office, *farmácias*. The problem was that when it was my turn to be served at least one Portuguese person would dart in front of me, and demand attention from the employees, sometimes interrupting me mid-sentence. I'll never communicate in Nina's nuance way, but thanks to Bruno, I now get the service I deserve. *Bow-wow!* I bark, *Get back! Get back in line! Wait your turn!* Even using English words I find that I am perfectly understood.

Standing outside the Serralves Museum waiting for a ride share I was backed into by a too-tan woman wearing too much gold jewelry. She had to have seen me. I´m fairly tall and was the only other person on the sidewalk. It´s hardly as if she was engrossed in professional work; she was photographing the iron gates with her cell phone. I barked a professional warning first, *Ola! Eu este aqui.* The woman could see that. When she yelled back at me *Não!* as if I was somehow at fault, I could have bitten her right then and there. There were no witnesses. I stiffened instead, dug my feet into the concrete and fixed her with the hard gargoyle stare. I actually learned this first from Portuguese people, but the madness in my eyes was pure Bruno. She moved.

Admittedly I was also peeved because she looked good in those tight, white pants. We seemed the same age, but I´d never attempt that look.

At a café that I frequent I ordered a breakfast sandwich of bacon and egg, asking for the egg *duro, não liquido* (hard not liquidy). When the plate arrived I lifted the bread to inspect the contents as usual and all I had to do was bark, *Arf! Arf!*

Arf! until the waitress came running to remove my plate, and reheat the gooey yellow egg. Naturally, I gave her a large tip. I then walked to the bank, where I admired the bank manager´s pen, and he sweetly slipped it into my envelope of cash. *Yip, Yip, Yip* I barked, channelling the joyful enthusiasm of Max, the lucky Jack Russell terrier. Possibly the other customers misunderstood that I'd been stabbed.

The misunderstandings when I try to actually speak Portuguese continue, when I least expect them to. I was in the Continente hipermarket and approached an employee who was arranging decorative pillows. I asked her where the bed pillows that were advertised on sale were, and she began screaming, *Não! Não!* and backing away as if I'd made her an indecent proposal. I had asked very nicely, *Desculpa, mininha, onde este almofadas com pele de frango?* I accompanied the request with mime, putting my palms together between my cheek and shoulder as if I was going to sleep. Now, I may have said something like,

Little girl, where can I sleep on pillows made with the skin of dead chickens? but in context it should have been perfectly clear.

So, now when I am ignored or misunderstood, and need something badly I simply bark more loudly. I don't exactly lick people with gratitude, but I do kind of jump up, and paw them. This has at times been misunderstood, so a PhD married to an MD told me that I should introduce myself from now on as *Doctor* to create distance, and decorum, because I have neither naturally.

On a warm spring day I see a Great Dane in profile sunning itself up on the fifth floor on a small balcony. It is leaning on its forearms on the balcony ledge, looking down on *Rua Nova de São Gens* and the post office, and the small, older shops. *Why am up I here?* It must be thinking. *Where did I go wrong?* I feel as confused as a Great Dane on a fifth-floor balcony much of the time. I've never understood for example why cities spend millions of dollars buying recycling centers and trucks and plastic bins as a solution to too much plastic. Why don´t they just outlaw plastic? Why refrigerators and washing machines fifty-years old still work, but new ones are made to be thrown away in five? Customer service now means being thrown into a mosh pit of other confused customers called a community, or searching for a list of frequently asked questions. Microsoft, Google, and Apple enter our personal computers at will to vandalize them. What other businesses sell essential products, then break into our homes and take away our personal things with impunity, and repeat offend? After buying the computer, the software, the internet, and the electricity to be able to use it, why can´t we be left alone? Cookies have been turned from treats to toxins. Artificial intelligence is the ultimate oxymoron. Our human thoughts and communications are being constantly redirected to fixed sets of primitive grimaces and grunts from emojis, beeps, dings and "fun" avatars.

HELLO, DOG!

Jaron Lanier says, *You are not a gadget.* George Lakoff says, *Always be on the offense. Never go on defense.* Bruno says, *Never be cowed (cãoed).* I´ve tried to be a good person all my life. In Portugal I learned to be a bad dog. That´s *Dr. Dog* to you.

Smoke rises from the balcony of the little taffy circus dog I watched in fascinated horror months earlier leaping desperately to the window on his bare apartment balcony to be rescued from a bitter, heavy rain. With no way to get to him, I feared the worst and turned away. He survived. His family got a table and chairs for the balcony. They are now BBQing. Nina has become mute. When I glimpse her through the *photinia* she is so fat that she can barely walk.

One day last spring a new sound filled the air. I saw Paulo out chain-sawing down the *photinia* between us. Seeing me eyeing the piles of branches he was dropping on my driveway he offered to pick them up. *I'll get them* I said twice, in a low growl. I've steered clear of Paulo ever since he attacked a man who was trying to deliver a reupholstered chair to me. The man had rung my buzzer. I'd just stepped out of a bath, and said I'd be there in a few minutes. Loud shouting began. I looked out to see Paulo, fists knotted lunging at the tiny elderly gentleman, who seemed twice his age, and half his size. I grabbed the nearest thing I could find, a bleach-stained purple bath robe, and threw it on as I ran down the steps dripping wet and out onto the sidewalk. Paulo became only more agitated when I asked him what was going on. He said the man had blocked his driveway. Paulo and his girlfriend have never parked in their driveway in the three years I have lived here. Soon he would make sure they never could. I explained the man was only there to drop off a chair. Still screaming Paulo grabbed the man's truck keys out of his hand, and climbed into the truck. Jumping back out, he threw the keys on the ground. The driver had said nothing. He got into his truck, and drove somewhere up the street and after a long while he came walking back carrying my chair. I

HELLO, DOG!

stood my ground dripping wet, barefoot, with nothing on but the ratty bathrobe. I refused to be cowed, or to be *cãoed*. (A Portuguese word for dog is *cão*.)

When he came back the delivery driver was shaking so badly I thought it best to not let him drive. I made him sit on the reupholstered chair in the open doorway next to the driveway. We drank two glasses of refreshing, chilled *vinho verde* and discussed the event loudly. My Portuguese vocabulary had grown surprisingly and was just full of choice words for the neighbor; *idiota, horrível, louco*. The driver used the word, *savage*. The same in Portuguese, English, and Old French, the word can mean *reckless, ungovernable,* and also, *tearing with the teeth*.

Over the next two days Paulo sent me at least a dozen text messages. "This is not a UNESCO heritage site!" "…your wallet and your mind" "Leave my family alone!" "You live with lies!" and, "Learn and respect courtesy!" The only meaning I could piece together from these random messages and this incomprehensible rage was that it was one thing for me to buy the most run-down house on the street, paint it, renovate its garden, replace its rusting fence gate panels, replace hazardous wiring and leaking plumbing, but coming into his neighborhood and buying chairs was too much for him to bear.

A few months later Paulo severed all fourteen of the *photinia* trees, ending what visual buffer we´d had. The *passeiro* nests swung limply before dropping to the concrete. It took him several days. One day I caught the spectacle of Paulo "tight-rope" walking along the narrow top of the high wall between our driveways, swinging a running chain saw like an action hero in a film. Framed in the window his girlfriend held her daughter in place on her lap. Smiles of feminine admiration for Paulo´s destructive capacity were frozen on their faces. The fourteen *photinia* trees still litter their driveway eight months later. Nina is now confined to an even smaller patch of concrete. I have no idea where she poops or pees. I have no idea where the *passeiros* now live, or if they are still performing as a choir.

These neighbors are nothing, and everything I wanted. I hope to be out of here by Christmas. I look night and day for a house with a bigger garden, with trees where song birds are welcome. I plot ways that I might take Nina with me. How much from *my estrangeira's wallet* might free her? Would he poison her if he knew I wanted her? Could a neutral animal rescue group intervene on her behalf? Probably not Isabel, who must continue to live next door to him.

On a warm day the window in the fifth-floor flat behind me that has a bird is open. The caged bird sings to those who are outside. I listen for a while as she waits for a response. When no bird answers, I answer. I speak as much bird as I do Portuguese.

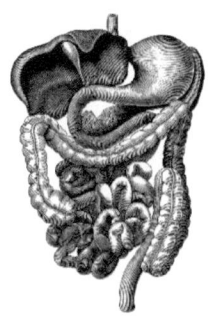

WEIRD FOODS OF PORTUGAL

I ordered the *prato do dia* at the traditional restaurant nearest my house. Sometimes I pass the owner out walking. We are on nodding terms. He must live close to me. Frankly, I do not like Portuguese cuisine, which is what he and his family make, and serve. Portuguese agriculture, *frutarias* three to a block, affordable local, heirloom fruits and veggies. Those are all things I love about Portugal! The cuisine? Well, we could start by adding a few herbs and spices and giving salt, sugar and olive oil a rest.

This neighbor is a barrel-chested man with a beatific face. With weary patience he gave me the day's menu options. I chose the fish, advertised simply as *pescada*. As I waited, I looked about. The restaurant is cheap and cheerful. It was recently renovated, and it has a large picture window that lets in lots of light. It is very clean, as most humble places in Portugal are also very clean. I walk here from my house in four minutes. When its doors are open everyone is welcome to enter and sit in this restaurant. This is one thing I admire about the place. People stake out seats forty minutes ahead of lunch, which begins at noon.

Now that I think of it, a lot of the regulars seem to be drunks. The weather-beaten men and the odd single woman who sit waiting with me have a stunned look - as if surprised that they woke up at all that morning, let alone with the unimaginable good fortune of being seated in a clean, sunny café waiting to be served a hot, freshly prepared meal. But these roughened customers have high standards, for in addition to the friendly service, the food here is great! The food is so great in fact, that twice I have lost my standards where it comes to what I will and what I will not eat. Let's just say the first time vampires would have approved of my transgression, and leave it at that.

The *prato do dia* comes complete with a drink. I never drink soft drinks, soda, pop, soda pop—whatever one chooses to call that synthetic, sugar-and-chemical-laced swill—so, I ordered the *vinho verde*, and smiled as the owner's mother - in her plaid apron, barrettes holding her curly grey hair back from her face - set down a chubby glass pitcher of *vinho* filled to the brim. She is just as pleasant as her son. As if I could possibly finish off a whole pitcher of wine at lunch! She also set down a basket of heavy, cornmeal *broa*. The *prato* soon followed. It featured white rice, three roasted new potatoes, a bowl of homemade cabbage soup with bits of red beans, and even tomato suspended in its potato-thickened broth, (an unusually chunky and appetising soup), and a separate stainless-steel platter. This is where my culinary reservations reared up.

Three snarling, fanged dragons glared up at me from the platter. Their snakelike bodies were coiled, ready to strike. Even frying had not diminished their terrifying appearance. They had jagged points all along their backs, huge heads, and oversized, mammalian eyes that would have been cute in a fluffy horse or camel, but were horrifying here. Camels are cantankerous and untrustworthy animals. Once one mistaking my hair for hay, or thinking this was somehow funny, almost ate out a chunk of it down to my scalp. (That was another continent, and another time.)

Later, to understand what I had been served as "lunch," I looked up the name for the points that travelled down the *pescadas'* serpentine spinal backs, and I came upon the Dimetrodon, an extinct reptile that lived about 300 million years ago during the Permian Period:

Dimetrodon means "two measures tooth," because the monster had two different kinds of teeth in its large skull.

The first set of teeth were designed to capture and hold prey. The second set of teeth were used to shear flesh from the bone. Judging from its teeth and jaw design, it's quite obvious to paleontologists that Dimetrodon was a meat eater.

Well, the creatures snarling up at me from the platter left no doubt in my mind what their culinary preferences were! Their predatory, flesh-rending teeth, sharpened to needle-like points were on full display. Camels and horses have big, flat topped, piano-key teeth, not these flesh-tearing weapons! Camels have double sets of eyelashes, not double sets of teeth!

It was no surprise to me that the man who discovered the Dimetrodon in 1878 is known as Edward "Drinker" Cope, because a drinker is what I quickly became. I refrained from grabbing the chubby pitcher of wine with both hands and guzzling from it directly, but did not stop pouring until the pitcher was dry. Perhaps it had been servings of this very delicacy on this very spot that had turned the other early diners from dewy-faced innocents into the red-faced regulars surrounding me now.

Nothing but the benevolent gazes of *senhor* and his mother, and the curious gazes of the other diners at the tall *estrangeira* in their midst could have kept me seated, pretending calm as I took up knife and fork to these monstrous creatures; their gawking eyes, writhing bodies, their abysmal jaws, and flesh-snagging, flesh-tearing prehistoric teeth. I took my time, as if admiring the perfect, light, golden breading. It appeared to be *milho*, innocuous cornmeal. It was nearly the color of a Golden Delicious apple. If only! Where was that precious fruit when I needed it?

My stomach went thought a panoply of emotions as my brain tried valiantly to hold it together: This restaurant is very clean. The owner and I must be close neighbors. He seems a kind man. As a former restaurant owner myself, I admire his ability to balance the responsibilities of wages, taxes, and electric bills and still come up with nutritious, balanced meals at prices that his customers can afford. His cook is charming in her tilted cloche. She steps out of her kitchen frequently to survey her customers´ enjoyment. She makes truly superior soup.

And, I was very hungry that day. I was fairly new in this neighborhood, and wanted to appear assimilated, so I sat up straighter in the wooden chair, and - as if it were nothing - using knife and fork I separated the flesh from the least threatening of the meat-eating monsters. I chose the one whose eyes were looking away from mine. Its head was down, as if trying to flush a bit of sand from its eye at the moment of death. Perhaps it had been shedding a tear that it would not live to see its son, Freddy grow up to take off his first fisherman's finger.

I tasted the mother's waist, and her chest area. Fine. Mild. White. Fish. A slight moistness, no gooeyness. The cook is absolutely skilled! Then, the other two creatures reared up glaring. They snarled at me again. I pushed the platter to the farthest edge of the table, and poured the last drops of *vinho* into my glass. I positioned the empty wine pitcher, the oil and vinegar cruets in their stand, and the bread basket between myself and the unspeakable platter. Grateful to have one last potato on my plate, I speared it into my mouth. I went to the register to pay, foregoing my usual coffee and fruit salad, even though they were included in the price.

The fish I later learned are not called Dimetrodon, but *marmotinha de rabo na boca* or, *pescadinhas de rabo na boca* or, *pescada* or just *hake*. They are also known as *verdinhos,* or *blue whiting. Hake* is my preferred word because it reminds me of the Haka war dance performed by New Zealand's national rugby team. If the *All Blacks* warriors ever need fresh inspiration for their intimidating grimaces they need only order a few platters of fried *hake,* and take notes. I recommend they order wine, as well.

After *hake,* the *francesinha* gets my vote for one of the weird foods of Portugal. Supposedly classified as a sandwich, this is something at which it fails miserably. I am somewhat qualified as a sandwich expert. Not only did I grow up in an Italian town in New Jersey renowned for *Del's Deli Sloppy Joes*, (a mixture of chopped ham and cole slaw heaped onto white sandwich bread, which budding chefs that we were, we topped with Fritos corn chips,) and the original *Mike's Subs*. I started *Mandy's Sandwiches*, a carry-out operation that grew into the *Catalpa Tree Cafe*, which became regionally famous for its own sort-of sandwich, the *Catalpa Tree Burrito*, which my business partner, Randal created. A decade later I revived my sandwich business at the request of a vegan bakery near my house. The bakery paid me mainly in barter for its cranberry-walnut and blueberry muffins, but these earned me social currency at my daughter's pre-school, and with the playgroup moms.

In graduate school in Sydney, Australia I ate mainly sandwiches, alternating between the banh mi bought for $4 from the Vietnamese stalls I passed when walking from Glebe to the Central Business District, and falafels I made at home from a boxed mix, rolling them into chewy Lebanese pillows of bread that cost $1 for four at the Harris Farms market. There were also the Vietnamese fresh rolls my friend, Cattie Cheung taught me to make, easy to transport in my backpack rolled up in wax paper, and put into a plastic bag.

These sandwiches were cheap, packed with flavor, crunch, and vitamins, and perfect to eat anywhere. To my mind, there is no meal more sublime than one that can be eaten without a plate, without utensils, held in one hand. That would not be the *francesinha*.

To be perfectly honest, I have eaten just one *francesinha*. To be even more honest it was advertised as, "vegetarian," or even as "vegan."

In Portugal this can mean the pork or beef has been replaced with chicken. Regardless, that one was enough. *Francesinha* is usually explained to mean *little French girl*. Obscene, cannibalistic connotations set aside – but just for the moment - nothing could be less like a child of any nationality than this hot mess on a plate. A large, French trollop of retirement age I can see, although I would prefer not to.

Around Porto, Portugal, billboards for hotels that bill by the hour are common. Most show a woman's face, her head thrown back in ecstasy. (Or in pain. It's hard to tell which. The billboards are not exactly finely drawn.) Lately, the billboard turning up the most frequently in front of schools and shopping centers shows a shirtless back of a man in snug-fitting blue jeans, his butt muscles clenched. Minimal, additional detail in front of the man suggests why his butt muscles are clenched.

The *francesinha*'s sodden mattress of white bread, and its odiferous gravy conjure nothing so perfectly as a romp on a filthy mattress where countless other beer drinkers have romped before. With its springs softened under the weight of ham, *linguiça*, sausage and beef, its blanket of greasy, melted cheese over which the dark bedspread of sauce is ladled, tasting as if it has been sweated out, one might consider the *francesinha* serves as the poor man's substitute for the hotel-by-the-hour experience. While an entire *prato do dia* including main course meat or fish, rice, potatoes, salad, soup, wine, coffee, and dessert typically costs under nine euros, the *francesinha* can cost €15 with nothing but a few soggy French fries tossed into the stinking gravy. The one redeeming quality of the *francesinha* that I can think of is that it can be eaten without unzipping your pants. However, you will need cutlery, and napkins a plenty.

Locals will have their favorite restaurant with the best Francesinha in town, typically arguing about the quality of the sauce (a secret recipe that varies by restaurant) and the quality of the meats. Each restaurant holds its sauce recipe in secrecy.

Well, why not keep it a secret! Who really cares to know what type of labor the gravy sweat exuded from, or which cuts of meat, or even which animals were turned into sausages and steak? How beneficial is it really to know whether swine, cow, horse, or retired trollop is lying on that slab of bread, or to know whether a regular cooking device warmed the runny egg, or if it was simply cracked open between two steamy, hot thighs? My question is about Daniel da Silva, who in 1953 invented the *franchesina* as, "Porto's answer to the Croque Monsieur." Was Daniel a witty satirist, or yesterday´s pedophile sowing revenge for rejected conquests in France?

Something very surprising turned up when I looked up this string of words: "Average cost and weight of a *francesinha*." The fifth-, sixth-, seventh-, eighth-, and ninth-place results were:

Gastric Sleeve Cost in Florida, Cost of Gastric Bypass Surgery in Florida, Bariatric Surgery Cost in Florida, Liposonix Orlando Florida, and *Tummy Tuck Cost in Jacksonville, Florida.* In the words of humorist Dave Barry, *I am not making this up.* It is of course comforting to know that my chances of ever requiring one of these medical procedures will be reduced if I never eat another *francesinha,* but it is weird that I lived in South Carolina, a stone's throw from Florida for thirty years, and I never heard of *francesinhas* being sold in the region.

Is it possible Portuguese clandestinely travel in such large numbers to Florida for this surgery, rather than expose any possible defect in their national cuisine that they have created this niche medical industry in anything-goes Florida? Are those "Disneyland" trips I´ve heard Portuguese bragging about loudly merely cover stories? If so, this would make the *francesinha* the world´s most expensive sandwich!

Florida has the *Cuban,* its own massive, redundantly meat-rich sandwich. At least Cubans have pickles for fiber. I've eaten Cubans from Florida's Publix grocery store chain, and they are good, and they can be held in one hand, and eaten without cutlery. If one eats too many, *"Disneyland"* is nearby if needed. It might be helpful to learn a few Portuguese phrases though to gain entry to this speakeasy surgery.

In the beach town of Matosinhos the front window of one typical-flavoured restaurant, *Sabor Tipico* is filled with stacks of firewood. Inside more firewood runs the length of the wall opposite the takeaway deli counters. I've chosen to eat the *Porco à Alentejana* from the deli here because I can pick out the pork and just eat the clams, potatoes, and pickled vegetables. I like pickled vegetables. As I waited I watched three men stagger in under loads of more firewood. It was sticky-hot July. I asked the waitress, "What is all this wood for?" She pointed to an arched iron oven door behind a small counter at one side of the dining room. "It is for the *francesinhas*. We set them in there for a few minutes to give them flavor," she said. Sure enough, twice during my meal the oven door was opened. I saw the yellow flames and red embers kept fed in the back of the cavern. Once, its door was opened to slide in a porcelain restaurant dish the waitress carried from the kitchen, and once it was opened to slide the dish back out again. I looked away. I knew what was on that dish.

I´m certain *Sabor Tipico* makes *francesinhas* to exactingly high standards, using the most hygienic methods, and high-quality ingredients. For anyone hankering for a trip to "*Disneyland*" I suggest that its *francesinhas* might be worth the trouble, if any are.

In the next installment of "Weird Foods of Portugal" we will explore the truly weird foods made by deviants of Portuguese society. I´m talking about nationals who have broken from the herd to create true vegan cheeses, veggie hot dogs, roasts of tempeh, and canapes of creamed *legumes* piped onto ruby slices of *beterraba* (beetroot). I´ve tried them all, and I can assure you these foods also pair well with *vinho verde* by the glass or the pitcherful. Thank God, Portugal is a pluralistic society!

Happiness Factory

I met Bette at opening time outside the gates to the Serralves Museum. The day sparkled. The air was fresh, and sweet. It was only February, but already pollen tickled the tips of tender, green leaves in the surrounding trees. Bette is the tiniest of Danes, living large in her mid-eighties. In recent years she has ridden an elephant in India, travelled alone to Ethiopia, visited the great museums of Europe. She will go almost anywhere without a thought. She plays golf, gardens and goes to the gym weekly. She reads voraciously in four languages. She likes art, and is opinionated about everything, and I love looking at art with Bette.

On this day we were twittering like birds. Eager to see the happy, primary-colored precise lines and shapes in an exhibit of art by Joan Miró. Inside we quickly became mute as we passed one coarse, frayed jute rope hanging after another. Literally, this was an exhibit of rotting hangman's nooses! From Miró's lynching series we shuffled on to his slash and burn series. We stopped in front of a grainy, black and white film of the rachitic old man slashing and setting fire to canvases as a bearded, young accomplice goaded him along. In disbelief Bette and I listened to some long-dead male announcer gushing enthusiastically over the artist's "technique," before we dragged ourselves onward. Finding ourselves alone in a secluded alcove beneath a white canvas slapped with a housepainter's brush dipped in black paint, Bette broke our silence. A guttural howl was followed by her bellow, "Look here!" This one he called 'Woman'! You have a breast here, an eye there! It was not enough for him to dismember her parts! He had to go back and cover her in black paint!"

Bette can be impulsive. To give you some idea, one stormy winter's day she suggested we take a stroll along the beach near her home, convincing me that this was normal behavior for a Dane. We stopped in front of the Capela do Senhor as the tide reached our feet. This is an ancient chapel set way out in the ocean on a slippery rock promontory. Bette noted that before it was a chapel it was a site of pagan sacrifices. I asked when we were getting the drinks in the warm café that she had promised. I´d humoured her already, and when she suggested we wade *out into the tide* now clawing at our ankles to get out to the promontory, I drew a line. In the sand. Which was promptly erased. The wind was gusting, drowning out my protests. Before I knew it Bette had disappeared into the fog. I had no choice but to dive in after her, find here, and grab onto her as her ballast as the waves pounded, and breached the low wall keeping us just barely from becoming *delícias do mar.*

Bette is as light as a feather. She could be on my shoulders in a flash. Then she'd demonstrate some slashing and burning techniques of her own. I'd be her accomplice. We had to get out of there quickly. I steered Bette out through the entering crowd toward a sandwich and a glass of wine in the museum´s outdoor garden tea house.

We've both been too many times to count to the Serralves museum, but in our state of agitation we kept getting lost. The museum grounds are 18 hectares of hills, lakes, and forests. We seemed to have tramped over all of them without seeing any sign of the tea house. Finally, we found ourselves deposited at a dead end of the path blinking at mounds of molding leaves and rusting wheelbarrow at a refuse heap. Panicked, we left the paths and began bushwhacking cross-country in what we hoped was the general direction of the tea house, clawing through any vegetation that happened to stand in our way. Suddenly our eyes were drawn upward by a flash of silver high up in the tree canopy. We headed that direction. Pushing through an inconvenient stand of old-growth oleander we fell out onto a giant teapot larger than Cinderella's pumpkin coach would have been. It was made out of welded curlicues of mouse-brown wrought-iron. It had a door, and the door was open.

We went inside and sat on two sun-warmed seats of the same smooth iron filigree. Gazing through our protective lace curtain of iron we looked across the garden at the biggest pair of high-heeled shoes we had ever seen. They were silver. Their heels alone were twice the height of Joan Miró.

After a while in the teapot we regained our calm. We felt ourselves again. We hopped like mountain goats over the ribbon-like fountain of turquoise tiles to get up close to the shoes. These were just cooking pots stacked in graduated sizes. I knew these pots. I had them in my own kitchen. They were the *Silampos Casserole, Low-Cost Model A*. Just behind the shoes was the sign we had looked for, Tea House, with an arrow. We savored our sandwiches and wine under the ivy on the old veranda.

Leaving the museum we ran into my friend, Cláudia arriving with her daughter. We warned them about Miró´s mutilation fantasies, and told them about the teapot and the shoes. Cláudia´s daughter told us the teapot and the shoes were made by a Portuguese artist, Joana Vasconcelos. Her show, "I'm Your Mirror" was replacing the dead Spaniard's. Minutes later Cláudia sent me this photo of the artist that she had just taken. It shows the artist in full-length black silhouetted against the cream marble floor working alone on a Sunday on her chandelier of pristine, white tampons, *A Noiva* (2001–2005). Curiouser and curiouser: Cláudia is a lighting designer. She gave me my first *Silampos Casserole, Low-Cost Model A*. And, Cláudia helped me make pristine white chandeliers for my home, although it never occurred to either of us to use tampons.

I'd never heard of Joana Vasconcelos before. Just her name seemed fantastical. One week later I read that Joana Vasconcelos was speaking at the Serralves - in 40 minutes. I'd been piddling around my house in old clothes. I pulled my hair back hastily into the gym scrunchie, and threw on a long yellow cotton skirt that I knew was clean because I pulled it out of the dryer. I slipped on the shoes I found next to the door, and raced out, arriving at the museum just in time to be seated by a young usher in one of the last remaining seats, which happened to be up front near the stage.

The artist was already on stage. She was seated in a low, curved-back armchair that made her appear slouching. Across from her sat an older gentleman. He began at once asking her questions, to which in response the artist hunched lower in her seat to manipulate a laptop computer on a low coffee table between them. As images of tempestuous beauty, fierce beauty blossomed behind them, the questions continued, but the questions seemed flat, pedantic, and not connected in any way to the startling images. The artist responded dutifully locating an image, and said as little as possible. It was almost as if she was a slightly resentful student or a daughter to the man.

The floor was opened for questions. I raised my hand. Apologising for speaking in English I asked, "Where does such a young woman find the courage to take such small, unimportant, traditional women's concerns and make them so big and important?" I said the American artist Judy Chicago was called a "pornographer" by the US Congress for her room-sized installation of dinnerware, *The Dinner Party* (1974–1979), and later told an interviewer that she made the piece room-sized as a statement because museums and galleries of that time were boycotting large art made by women. Applause erupted behind me as soon as I finished my question. I turned around in shock to see the whole audience applauding.

The artist wiggled to sit up straighter. She announced that she would answer in English. "That is a hard question to answer," she began.

"First, I am not so young. I am forty-eight. I was in a karate class at age eight. There were originally two other girls in the class, but they dropped out. I stayed in. And, I am not afraid. And, I am not afraid of scale." After a pause she said, "But I do ask myself, 'Why? Why me? Why am I the only woman, or the first woman, again, and again?'"

No one offered her an answer. The audience was now fidgeting. There many children with their parents. Still clutching school books, they needed to get home and be fed. The audience soon disbanded, but the artist's candour lingered in the air. It felt fiercely innocent.

I was in the lobby looking for a bathroom. An elevator opened in front of me. An impeccably dressed man in a grey suit stepped out, stopped and peered at me quizzically. He asked if he might be of assistance. Suddenly, I realized how sloppy I must have looked. I must have appeared to be mentally challenged. I raked my fingers through hair that had fallen out of my scrunchie, and looked down at my shoes, mumbling something about the bathroom. In horror I noticed the grey, thick, rind of dried mud caked all around my shoes, the childish bright yellow shoes I wear only working in the garden. The man brightened instantly, launching into detailed directions to not one, but two women's bathrooms. He practically listed the number of steps to each one. When I asked which of the two women's bathrooms he preferred, he blushed deep red, and admitted that he hadn't actually been *in* either one. I asked then if he worked for the museum. "I work for Joana," he said, presenting me with a glossy white business card. In the center of the card was a jack from the children´s game of Jacks, but in primary colors. "My name is Rui Silvestre," he said, "Like *Sylvester* Stallone."

Almost no one seemed less like the bleeding, rough, sweating, American action hero from *Rocky* films than this slim and dapper man standing before me. But his unexpected reference may begin to explain what happened next. Rui could make a cat discuss the history of art, and the quality of the lamb in German vs. Portuguese cat foods. I'm much easier. We were deep in discussions - religion, national politics, international politics, food, housing prices - all the usual topics with quick, non-sequitur redirects Portuguese excel at - when the artist sidled up. She was accompanied by a tall young man carrying a black garment bag, and the interviewer. They all stood silently listening attentively. Rui paid them no attention. He kept peppering me with questions until I became increasingly uncomfortable that these three other people had not been introduced or included. Not knowing what else to do, I stepped away from Rui, and over to Joana, where I made a crude chopping action next to her head, and said I would like to do karate with her.

The security guards all around us were yawning. In the United States of America, I'd be on the ground, tased and spasming, foot on my neck by now. (Maybe these guards knew that Joana had led an elite corps of night club bouncers trained in the martial arts at one time.)

Joana has the open, guileless face of a young girl. As one of the world's foremost plastics artists (which I only learned now does not mean she only works with plastics) she looked me over like she might size up a stack of pig iron bars. "You can do yoga with me," she said. "Ok, when?" I asked her. "Any Monday you can come to my atelier." The guards had been circling us tighter, looking ostentatiously at their watches. They wanted us to leave, so we went outside. I cannot tell you what we talked about outside, because what I remember is the moon. The sky was an inky blue-black. A wide, white, hazy path circled the moon. I was watching myself skate around the path around that moon, around and around. I heard Rui ask me to call him whenever I wanted to visit the atelier. I agreed. We parted for the night.

Nine days later I am standing in front of the address for the atelier that I was given. It is supposed to be at Lisbon´s Alcântara waterfront. I am standing in front of what looks like an enormous grey battleship that fills the entire block. I can't find any door or any sign, though. Finally, I find a small door painted in the same battleship grey. I see a small sign; *Atelier Joana Vasconcelos.* I see a buzzer, but when I buzz it several times no one comes, so I walk to the end of the block. Behind the ship I see a few small fishing boats bobbing in a bit of sea. The atelier is a building built on the banks of a small marina. This side is all glass. This side has a door, and the door is open. I go inside and find myself standing facing a wall of grey marble. There is no one around. In front of the wall is a low counter stacked with black rubber meal trays and white ceramic dishes, and soup bowls. On a long lower shelf are large bowls holding fresh fruit. A few folding dining tables are set up to my left.

It is completely silent here. Shards of sunlight travel the room, skip-glancing off the water ripples outside. They land on a string of glistening red ceramic chorizo sausages, and green and white onions, and a grey fish that looks just pulled and squirming from a river, and the red steer's head the size of a large boule of bread that I recognize as faience made by the Portuguese ceramics company, Bordallo Pinhiero. They are what I consider to be expensive. Yet, here they are arranged haphazardly on the wall as a kid might arrange found objects - bird feathers and driftwood - in her bedroom.

Behind me a thin young man with gingery short hair enters wearing a butter-yellow button-down shirt. He nods at me once and takes a banana from one of the bowls before disappearing through an open door at the far end of the room. There I notice a purple sofa with a large, knitted painting over it in vivid yarns tufted with walnut-sized pearls. A free-standing cube version of the panel sits next to the sofa looking slightly faded and squashed as if used as an outdoor play structure. (Researching this story, I learn a similar knitwork panel by the artist sold in 2015 for three million dollars.)

A three-spigot espresso machine is winking at me from a passage between the marble counters. As I'm considering if I might coax coffee from the machine without breaking it or getting caught a woman with hair like a full cone of cotton candy spun of molasses enters through the open door at the end of the room. She is wearing giant, square plastic eyeglasses and her face is a serene oval the colour of *meia de leite* (coffee with milk.) She giggles in surprise at seeing me, then slips behind the counter and the wall, returning with a *bica*-sized woman the color of *cheio*, who offers me a coffee. There is uncanny mind-reading here. I ask for a double *abatanado*, and the women retreat behind the wall leaving me alone with my coffee. I am in blissful silence with the sunlight, the sausages, the ships and my coffee until I take the first sip, and begin gagging and coughing violently on the mountain of cinnamon I´d dumped over the rim of my cup. (Please note: This is not my fault. Like most things here, the cinnamon shaker is oversized. Its holes are sized for granules of parmesan cheese, not cinnamon.) The *bica* woman reappears like magic to press a glass tumbler of water into my palm before disappearing again silently. (Apparently this is not the first time this has happened.) As I drink I admire the glass; it's heft, its sparkling thick faceted bottom.

I am still red-faced and teary-eyed when Leonor, a young employee Rui has arranged to give me a tour before yoga, arrives. I slug down the bitter sludge, declining a fresh cup because I know cinnamon is good for blood sugar regulation, and also, I'm too proud and not wasteful. Leonor plays with the ends of her shoulder-length blond hair as I swallow the paste. She wears thick glasses that make her eyes look soft and enormous. She has a tiny, discreet nose ring. She tells me that she was born and raised in Lisbon, and that she has degrees in art and in marketing. She takes my cup to the kitchen behind the wall, and we pass through the open door at the far end of the room.

We enter what looks like an airplane hangar repurposed as a hospital triage ward. Yellow hazard tape marks an area containing cot-like rows of bandage-wrapped sculptures. Standing guard outside this section is a cement garden lion sentry wearing armour of ripped, mauve-colored cotton crochet. Next to the sentry is a *Silampos Low-Cost Model A* shoe broken into two. It´s smaller than the ones at the Serralves, but still, sized right for a charm bracelet circling an arm the size of a tunnel. "Climbed on by a tourist," deadpans Leonor. At the right side of the hangar tall screens of pleated cloth partly conceal what looks like an operating table, with tall monitoring machines. This turns out to be where the art is photographed. The table rotates.

We enter another open doorway and are now in the heart of the atelier. A dozen artisans work around a wide communal table heaped with mountains of riotous color. Yarns in saturated red; ruby, garnet, magenta, and fuchsia, in citron yellow, in emerald green, mustard, gold, ultramarine blue, and amethyst purple jostle each other for attention, although the room itself is remarkably quiet especially for the number of people working together in such open space. The floors and walls are painted battleship grey. High up clerestory windows the size of mattresses pour sunlight on the artisans, and frame chunks of blue sky, clouds, and an occasional sailboat mast. There is none of the drama or frenzy of fashion ateliers depicted in movies like *The September Issue.*

We walk between the table and a seven-foot tall, open-top wall of drawers covered in black velvet. Each is labelled with a sample of its contents.

This is where the oversized baroque pearls in mauve, oyster, and pale blue that are used to tuft the artist's large knitworks are kept. Other drawers hold Chinese red, and bottle green glass-beaded sartouche trims. Drawers display cornsilk yellow and baby blue rayon-silk tassels the size of babies´ feet. Artisans pull out earbuds as we approach them. Leonor encourages me to touch everything, to ask the them any questions. I am too bedazzled by the colors and textures to speak. My fingers search out the intricate stitches on the pieces the artisans hold out to me eagerly to touch. They know that their work will travel the world to its top museums, galleries, and private collections, and they are justifiably proud.

I spy the giggling, oval-faced coffee goddess sitting a little ways away on a stool. One can´t miss that high crown of hair! She is hand-stitching a heavy, vanilla-colored fabric. With each stitch she pulls herself up tall with the long thread to tighten it precisely. The fabric is spilling over her lap, cascading across the floor.

It passes a small huddle of standing engineers hunched over large sheets of paper. Leonor lifts a long tube of the fabric, and I cry, "Oh! It's an octopus!" Not a brilliant guess, considering that since the Manueline period Portuguese artists have been inspired by the sea. "It is a *Valkyrie!*" Leonor corrects, "Six arms, not eight!"

Vasconcelos's *Valkyries* are inspired by the thirteenth-century flying Norse warrior-goddesses, and by real women. This is *Egeria,* named for the fifth-century wandering Iberian cartographer. Her arms will be inflated to fly over a Barcelona shopping center. The engineers are now studying her complex cabling system. We wander next down to the basement machine shop where the warm smell of oil mixes with sharp tang of wood shavings. We share a few words with the atelier carpenter and machinist standing before a wood lathe sized to turn house pillars before we head back to the main atelier floor, and onto a ramp I had not noticed before. It is a gentle, nautilus spiral wide enough for riding golf carts. At the top is Rui in a small, glass-walled office. He is working alone, unlike anyone else I've seen here, and he appears stressed. He is preparing for a meeting so we move on.

Outside Rui's office a hallway is lined with conjoined glass-walled rooms. The first we enter is like a children's discovery museum. Models of works currently under production, and spare parts of finished pieces line shelves along the walls. Colorful architectural plans and spreadsheets are thumbtacked to the walls. They track more than one hundred projects scheduled for delivery around the world. We play with a small working motor, and I pick up a pressed glass tumbler just like the one presented to me in the café to stop me from choking. (Later, at the Serralves Museum I will see this tumbler by the hundreds married to striated automotive wheels, which welded together form the perfect Art Deco filigree wedding band for a glittering diamond solitaire Vasconcelos calls *Solitário*

[2018]. This is a love token so big people that walk through it as if under a wedding bower).

Next to the drinking glass on its own table is a three-tiered wedding cake with butter cream icing topiary and figurines attired in 18th century livery all made of ceramics. This is a model for a three-story wedding cake that will function as a working pool house for a very famous French family on their very famous historic estate.

The cake pool house, and final pool house, and everything Vasconcelos does is made, designed, tested, built, photographed, and/or shipped from this waterfront studio by its sixty employees, or else made in one of Portugal's traditional factories. The cake pool house, the swimming pools glazed with the artist's loopy, swooping colorful marker doodles, which have been made for municipalities as well as private estates, and the thousands of curved jigsaw pieces throbbing thirty meters in the air like a beating heart for *Coeur de Paris* (2018), commissioned as functional lighting for Paris' Clingancourt Metro station are all made at the Lisbon ceramics factory, Viúva Lamego founded in 1849.

The Silampos stainless steel casseroles elevated as high-heeled art first at the Palais de Versailles, and then at the Venice Biennale were made in a small town in Portugal at the Silampos factory founded in 1951.

Leonor leads me up another small back staircase to a sunny cubby. We meet two lace-makers with crochet hooks threaded with cotton. A laughing brunette with snapping brown eyes lays down her hooks threaded with black that she is building over a red ceramic crab the size of a footstool. She tells us, "Women always did this. They could not work outside the home, but they wanted to do something to keep busy, so they made this." Her grandmother and her mother were lace makers in Lisbon. Her young colleague across the table continues to struggle to fit her ecru lace over the ear curves of a life-sized calf's head. Gesturing with her chin toward her mentor she says, "I learned from her." Portuguese women did not typically keep busy by covering ceramic animals with lace. That brainstorm was Vasconcelos.'

I discovered Bordallo Pinheiro in the mid-1990s only because the company was struggling, and I was able to pick up a green cabbage leaf plate with a tiny frog at a US home goods discounter for €6. (Twelve years later my daughter smuggled it in her suitcase to college, and she still uses it in her grown-up home as a soap dish). The young Vasconcelos was beginning her art adventures. The Portuguese company founded in 1884 by popular cartoonist Raphael Augusto Bordallo Pinheiro was barely eking out survival by mass-producing small consumer ware, much of it unbranded for other companies. Vasconcelos discovered that the molds for its large, phantasmagorical Art Nouveau insects and beasts had been carefully mothballed decades earlier by a forward-thinking employee. She began commissioning the big creatures, coddling them one by one in traditional handmade lace. She saved them from extinction. "Joana is widely credited with saving the company from bankruptcy," says Leonor.

It is time for yoga. Leonor hustles me up one more hidden staircase, and I enter a small dressing room where two other women are just finished changing. We hang our things on simple wooden pegs on the wall, and walk a few more steps up to a skylit attic room. Five or six people are seated cross-legged, stretching, or are gathering heavy, white muslin sacks from a pile that reminds me of sandbags the city of Charleston, South Carolina gave out before hurricanes. The instructor, Iliana, a tall, willowy, robust and gorgeous woman perhaps in her early forties arrives. She introduces herself, and helps me to arrange a sandbag under my back. Forty minutes go by like no time at all, as we drape ourselves almost effortlessly over the sacks, following Iliana's gentle suggestions. Somehow by the end of the class we are flushed, energized, lightly covered in sweat, without anyone twisting us or telling us that we are not doing it correctly. Nothing was complicated.

Joana was not in attendance, which I think was a shame because I think she would have liked it. I linger talking with Iliana then take the wrong staircase back to the dressing room, nearly colliding with Joana, who is charging up the steps two at a time pursued by a ferret-like woman in a no-nonsense, grey business suit. We say hello self-consciously. I´m sweaty and embarrassed. We continue our separate ways. Leonor finds me. She has been searching for me, and tells me I must hurry, and dress quickly because I am supposed to attend the meeting with Joana and Rui! Leonor waits outside the changing room as I throw on my street clothes.

She leads me down to the main atelier floor where Rui and Joana, the small woman in grey, and another man are standing in front of the artisans still working quietly. The small group acknowledges me, and parts to let me into the circle, as Leonor whispers in my ear: The small woman is an important Gulbenkian Museum Board Director. "How are you?" asks Joana as I enter their circle. Flushed with endorphins all I can manage to get out is one word: *Happy*. Joana beams as if I have given her the one present that she has wanted for most of her life.

Joana's smile is similar to *Mad* magazine's Alfred E. Newman character's smile, if Alfred was a beautiful woman with perfectly applied lipstick. Joana's smile makes her look like someone it would be a lot of fun to get into trouble with. A lot of trouble. "That's good!" she says, "*You* should always be happy!" She strangely emphasizes the word *you*. I consider this with the newly expanded mind of one who has just completed a very good yoga class. If the woman who has made a factory dedicated to making happiness says that I should always be happy, maybe she is right.

Regaining some verbal capacity I say, "I have to tell you, the atelier reminds me of a commune." I had meant this as a compliment. The Gulbenkian Board Director rears back in horror. Swivelling to Joanna she demands, "No one sleeps here, do they?" I try to explain, "I don't mean a 'wild sex' sort of commune…." I am about to say that what I mean is a sober, enterprise-driven commune like an organic farm, but Joana has taken the matter into her own capable hands. "That maybe," she says. "We don't rule that out." She means the sleeping. Possibly she means some type of commune.

Today Joana is dressed in all white. She looks particularly regal, except that she is struggling to keep a straight face.

She then asks what Leonor has shown me. She asks me my impressions of what I have seen, and she waits for and considers my answers. When I chide her (mildly) for missing yoga, she expresses wistful regret, explaining she was required to prepare for this meeting. Then she says, "You must visit my therapist." I´m taken aback. I'm dishevelled from yoga, and dressing so quickly. I'm naturally not looking my best. Do they really think there is something wrong with me mentally? Was this visit intended as some sort of intervention? Am I to be reinvented by the plastics artist, not as a teapot, or a pair of shoes, but as some better vision of myself? Joanna repeats her suggestion that I visit her therapist, then without another word to anyone she turns and floats away like a fluffy, white cloud in a blue sky, with the Gulbenkian Board Director stepping quickly to catch up to her.

Leonor has her orders. I follow her reluctantly with a quick goodbye to Rui and the other fellow. We descend into the basement. I have no idea what is going to happen next. The therapist is a large, dark-skinned woman with huge, probing, dark eyes. She begins asking me questions about myself. I deflect these by asking her, *What are your medical credentials?* Well, it turns out she has a quite a long list of medical credentials. As she recounts her years of education, her advanced specialty coursework, her residencies at various institutions, I scan her office. I am somewhat relieved to see what might be a massage table, and realize at some point that Joana had simply invited me to have a massage.

I've had my clothes off at the atelier once already today, then possibly started a rumor about it becoming a "wild-sex" commune, so I decline. Instead, I follow Leonor up to the first room I entered, the sunny room on the harbour. There the *bica* woman who saved me from a choking death is waiting with a delicious lunch buffet of quinoa, chicken, cooked vegetables, and salad. She offers me another coffee after I've eaten, which I also decline, not wanting to interrupt the peaceful sound of lapping of water, and my quiet conversation with Leonor. We kiss goodbye, promising to keep in touch. I walk around the building to the parking lot to meet the ride-share car I have contacted.

A white Kia is waiting for me. The driver is a bouncy young woman named Susana. She has frothy blond hair, and wears a striking, black cotton peasant blouse embroidered extravagantly in silky red thread. I compliment her, telling her that her blouse reminds me of needlework I've just seen being made inside the atelier. She tells me the name of the shop where she bought the blouse, and describes many of the other wonderful things the shop has to offer. There are cute dresses, and great cowboy boots! This is all helpful and nice and all, but I am vibrating with my experience. I cannot contain it much longer. As soon as Susana stops talking about the boots she saw at the shop, I gush, "I can't believe my luck, being invited to the atelier! I just suggested karate as a joke!" I continue in this vein, (probably repeating myself) until Susana turns in her seat. If she had not needed both hands to steer the car down the highway we were driving she would have thrown them up in the air. "Well, of course she invited you! She is friendly! She is Portuguese!" she explodes. Susana seems exasperated that I could possibly be so blind as to miss something so obvious.

A few weeks later at the Casa da Música cafe I run into a friend of a friend talking with another member of the orchestra. She is talking with the tuba player, a man who wears a knitted stocking caps during rehearsals, which I often attend with friends. I ask them if they've seen the Vasconcelos exhibit. In response, the tuba player pulls out his phone, and thrusts it at me. The screen shows a photo of a giant penis. It looks like a balloon. I ask him if he thinks Vasconcelos has made this penis, and he shakes his stocking-capped head vigorously, and says, "Yes." There is no way that Vasconcelos made this penis. A Vasconcelos penis would be richly detailed, not this amateur junk. "Why don't you like her?" I ask. He grumbles about the artist receiving too much of other's tax dollars. I´m too much in shock to ask how much of his salary and his rehearsal space are supported by tax dollars.

Vasconcelos pays homage to the six thousand Portuguese businesses registered in the textile trade with her columns of hissing steam irons, *A Todo O Vapor*, (2012). It can also be seen as an homage to the professional class of *empregadas*. It is my favorite Vasconcelos piece, for the towers resemble giant green and purple Venus flytraps, and the towers make people jump, and laugh nervously when they move in syncopation, hissing hot steam. Vasconcelos drives a Piaggio Ape-50 from the holy site of Fatima to Lisbon hauling plastic religious statues for *www.fatimashop.* (2002) and honors her country's Roman Catholicism, and also its mom-and-pop, small businesses culture. The Ape, Italian for bee, a creature highly regarded for its industry, was designed after WWII as low-cost transport for moving goods. It is still used for short distances. A battered blue Ape-50 makes deliveries to the commercial center in my neighborhood. A video portion of her art piece shows the artist's harrowing 18-hour trip in her three-wheeled tut-tut powered by a Vespa scooter engine, protected only by God as a monstrous 18- wheeled truck bears down on her.

"Don't you love our food?" is the first thing locals ask foreigners in Portugal. Where families congregate weekdays to lunch over home-cooked meals, cooking casseroles, tea pots, and drink tumblers are much bigger than only women's concerns. The stainless-steel casseroles Vasconcelos turns into shoes reference also Portugal's $5.75 billion dollar shoe export trade.

I am back at the Serralves Museum pondering her pristine white tampon chandelier, wondering what possessed her to string together 15,000 tampons. The shape is familiar, known as the *Montgolfier* named for two French brothers who named the hot air balloon – and tellingly, the hot air that lifts balloons - after themselves. Surely, it was not bloviating brothers Joana was thinking about. With a little research I learn that the brothers lifted the balloon design from a Brazilian prodigy who studied and taught and invented many things in Portugal. His name was Bartolomeu Lourenço de Gusmão, and he demonstrated and published his balloon design 74 years before the brothers claimed to invent it. Why tampons? I don't know. I do know that I would never have known about this fascinating mathematician, linguist, herbalist, Jesuit priest, University of Coimbra professor, dreamer, inventor of flying machines and many more things, including the hot air balloon without Joana Vasconcelos.

I catch up again with Joana and Rui at the Serralves Museum at a mid-afternoon panel discussion. I've invited an American friend to join me, and I carry an oversized white paper shopping bag emblazoned with the red carousel logo of the 60-year-old toy shop, *Magic em Porto*. Inside the bag are thank-you gifts for Rui and

Joana. The discussion is one of those lovely cultural events that Portugal provides its citizens for free. Vasconcelos shares the dais with Petra Joos, Chief Curator of the Guggenheim Museum-Bilbao, Spain, and University of Porto Professor of Art, Isabel Pires de Lima. Pires de Lima discusses a history of women in art. Petra Joos states, "Joana's exhibit was the most beautiful exhibit the museum has ever hosted. People ask all the time when it is coming back. Families came with their children. This is not so usual." Joos strikes me as someone who is not prone to hyperbole. Joana again says little, seeming unwilling to talk about herself.

Rui Silvestre catches my eye afterwards, and waves me over to him, where I introduce my friend and tell him about her book of fiction that takes place in Lisbon. I hand Rui the big bag, and his eyes light up behind his fashionable eyewear. "I wasn't expecting this!" he exclaims. He tears into the bubble wrap that was lovingly piled on by the toyshop's employees. Here is Sylvester

Stallone. I´m watching *Rocky* pummelling that plastic as if his future depends upon it.

When Rui has freed the toddler-sized head of wooden Pinocchio his eyes become gentle again. "It's hand-made in Italy," I explain. "It wasn't expensive. You were the only person I saw working alone at the atelier so I thought maybe you could use an office mate." "Ha!" snorts Rui, "Normally my office is *filled* with people." He returns to demolishing the wrapping, then sits his liberated little pal´s bottom on his forearm. He cradles the puppet-boy´s head in his neck. "You can bounce ideas off him," I say, "He can even speak to you if you are lonely. For example, he can say, 'I'm a real boy! I'm a real boy!'" For this part I use the plaintive, high-pitched hollow voice that I imagine Pinocchio has. Rui looks at Pinocchio as if he is a real boy, and coos and murmurs over and over, "I never expected this. I never expected this….I felt bad that day that I had not spent more time with you…."

Joana has noticed the commotion from across the room. She waves and makes her way over through a small crowd of fans. "Hi!" she says cheerfully, "I did not realize you would be here." I introduce my friend to her, plugging her book again, and hand Joana the tiny white bag containing a cheap, solar-activated dancing heart toy. (What can I really give Joana Vasconcelos?)

Today Joana wears raspberry-colored lipstick that complements her dark hair and fair skin, and a light purple caftan in soft-looking cotton gauze. Someone on the museum's staff tugs her sleeve. She has to go for photos. I ask my friend, who is never without her camera around her neck and for whom I have taken photos at every event she has invited me to if she has taken any photos, and she says, no, it never occurred to her. She sees two other friends across the room, one I've met a few times. I say goodbye to Rui, and follow her across. We reach the others, and my friend announces that they have made plans that do not include me. She uses those words.

Susana the ride-share driver is right: Joana is friendly, and Joana is Portuguese. I´m beginning to think Joana's art is about being friendly and being Portuguese. Spinning candy-colored plastic picnic ware into the filigree hearts traditionally made of silver and vermeil, and spinning these to fado music to celebrate Amália Rodrigues´ rags-to-riches life, (*Independent Heart*, 2008) is ingenious. Turning pig iron into comforting lace as a teapot with open doors is ingenious. Ingenuity is a Portuguese trait. Farm workers, factory workers, dressmakers are all ingenious. A persecuted priest invents aviation. Women cartographers map wild lands. And, an unkempt woman in muddy shoes gets remade as a pampered guest who can answer the question, "Why me?" *Why not you, Joana?* Why not any of us?

A Secret Soldier

Northern Portugal limps toward spring through a soggy, sepia melancholy. I'd found the most lavish bath towels I could find to force-bloom things along. They were watermelon color, Portuguese-made. I bought a whole set.

The overstuffed paper bags were disintegrating in a light drizzle as I waited outside for the taxi. The car pulled up at an angle. To avoid hitting a car parked along the street or spilling my beautiful things into its muck, I grabbed the front door handle, straddled the muddy rivulet, opened the door wide as I could, and flung myself plastered and dangling with packages into the front seat of the car. The driver was a small man with a head of close-shaven grey hair. He barely glanced up as I apologized for invading his private space, but he brushed off my apologies in perfect English. I had wine and oranges from the Algarve crammed into my blue patent leather messenger bag, which I juggled on my lap with the open top grass Morrocan basket overflowing with more Algarve oranges, and Azorean pineapple. The damp bags of towels I arranged around my feet, being careful not to pierce the fragile paper when I slipped the umbrella´s bayonet-like point between them. The driver sat stiffly at attention all this time, looking straight forward.

When I was finally settled, and strapped in under his seatbelt the driver squinted into his rear-view mirror. He asked where I was from, and what I did. I told him I was from the United States, and that I was writing. "I write also," he said, "but what I write no one can see." With this curious declaration hanging in the humid air, the driver stepped on his gas pedal. We entered the stream of cars pouring from Boavista´s rotunda in Friday´s late rush hour.

We drove lacquered streets in silence. I was thinking about a documentary I´d seen the night before shown at the Oporto Tennis and Cricket Club to a group of mainly retired Portuguese, American, and British expats. The film was by the BBC, and about the Irish General Wellesley, who defeated Napoleon at the Battle of Waterloo. It thought it was good, and reasonable as a topic of conversation with an older Portuguese gentleman, so I asked the driver if he´d seen it. I repeated the general's famous quote, "Next to a battle lost, the greatest misery is a battle gained."

The driver hadn´t seen it, but expressed polite interest. He said he knew who General Wellesley was, and that, "He was in Portugal." After a pause he said sharply, "I disagree with General Wellesley. A general can say that, a soldier doesn't." Silence again filled the cab until I suggested – genially, or so I thought - that maybe someone who'd lost a limb, or lost a friend in battle might agree with the general. The driver looked directly at me for the first time. "I have no leg, " he said. "From my knee to my foot are gone."

It was mercifully a short trip. As we pulled in front of my house, I snuck a quick peek at his legs. They were thin under khaki twill slacks. I wondered if his real leg, or his fake leg had operated the gas and the brake pedals. The story of a former roommate I hadn´t thought of in years came flooding back to me. It happened around 1980 in St. Louis, Missouri when the roommate was in a rough neighborhood at night, and a tough-looking gang of boys approached him. Propitiously, his prosthetic leg fell off. This sent the boys scurrying.

The roommate´s bedroom was just above mine in a sunny four-bedroom farmhouse we rented on the edge of the university town of Columbia, Missouri. Every weekday morning at 6 am I was awoken by a loud thumping overhead when the roommate got up and ready to leave for his nursing job at the Veterans Administration Hospital. After the weather warmed up, I saw him wearing shorts for the first time, khaki twill shorts, as a matter of fact. The thumping made sense, though he was still annoying. He had a fleshy-looking, molded fiberglass prosthetic leg, and hopped to the bathroom before strapping it on. For some reason I pictured the driver's as thin, cold, blue steel engineered for precision driving.

The streetlight in front of my neighbors´ house illuminated the inside of the cab, if dimly. António was 80, the robust, firm-hand shake 80, who did his own hedge trimming, and pressure-washing and came over with tools when I asked him, and one day redelivered two cases of wine to me on his own trolley, wearing a workman´s cap, held out waiting for a tip. I was laughing so hard I could barely open the carton to give him two bottles. His daughter, Elsa was hilarious, too.

Their chestnut tree now whipped over the streetlight in a frenzied dance, casting an erratic strobing effect into the cab. The rain was drumming down heavily. I was riveted to my seat; the wine bottle, the heavy fruits. The mushy bags of towels were pressed tightly around my feet and ankles. The umbrella's hard plastic handle hit my rib cage whenever I moved forward. I sat back. "Okay," I said. "What happened? And, why can't you show others what you write?"

The driver asked if I minded if he smoked, and when I said it was fine, he took a tiny filter that glowed white, and fit it into a gun metal-colored holder. "It's electronic. They say it's better for you," he said. He rolled his window down a crack. He began, "I was in Angola. My family thinks I was working as an engineer. I have no regrets." Studying the dancing tree, he took a puff at the window´s edge before turning back into the cab. "The thing is, you never look at a man you are killing," he said. "You think of them as a thing, not a man." I nodded as if this was the most common knowledge in the world. In a way, to me it should be. For my entire life my country has been killing people all over the world. It´s probably what America does better than anyone else, at least in terms of quantity. A quality death would probably involve old age, right?

I really knew nothing about it. Of course, I wanted to hear the driver's story. He continued, "There were these boys who always followed us around selling us cigarettes. The boys were pushing, grabbing, shouting, 'Buy me! Buy me!'" The driver leaned over and pinched a bit of my raincoat fabric to demonstrate. "There was one small boy alone. This young one didn't say nothing. He just stood there. So, I walked over to him. He had cigarettes, so I bought cigarettes from him. I don't know if he was six, or seven, or nine, because he always told us different numbers. Probably he did not know himself. He was probably the youngest." The driver took a puff out the crack. He turned back. "From then on, he lived with us. He lived with my men and me. He had an aunt who more or less took care of him, but she had seven or eight other children to care for so really she could not. From then on, where I went, Pelé went with me. Pelé is what we called him."

The driver was looking at me. His eyes were huge, very white. He was willing me to remember that day with him, and I did. From inside the dark cab under a pounding, cold rain I felt a blinding white heat of a noon in Angola. I saw a gaggle of wizened little boys. Most barefoot, skinny, bare chests rising from mis-sized, and faded shorts. The smallest boy stood apart. "They asked me to teach the soldiers," continued the driver, "I said, 'No!' I wanted no part of this! It was none of my business! I did my military service like all Portuguese males - two years. I had a son and a wife in Portugal! My parents were in Portugal, also. But they kept asking me." He looked back out the window and sucked hard on his device. He turned back to me and said, "A drop of water changed everything." I looked confused, I´m sure. "It's like this," he said, lifting both hands. I noticed they were fine-boned, expressive, hands.

"You have a glass of water up to the top." He cupped his hands around an imaginary vessel. "One drop more spills it over," he dropped his hands down the side of the vessel like a bird´s wings spent from flight, or like lava flow from a volcano. "So, I agreed to teach the soldiers. On two conditions. One, they give me Angolan citizenship, so I will not be a mercenary. And two, they pay me the same as the other captains. So, I was a captain. Both sides were terrible," he added after a puff. "I didn't like either one. They were like robbers and murderers. So, I worked for the robbers." *When was this?* I asked. "1986."

My mind wandered. Was he teaching in a classroom? Or, was it a jungle clearing, squatting in a circle in the dirt, drawing with a stick? Did the Angolan student soldiers wear uniforms like the Citadel Military College Cadets, who I sometimes drank iced tea with in their canteen when working near their campus? Their Delft-blue trousers and pale grey shirts made them look like country club parking valets. I couldn't picture it. Instead, I pictured Pelé, the Brazilian soccer player who flew across television screens in the 1970s and 1980s. His dark, somber face would light up each time he made a goal. Recently I´d read that Pelé - now age seventy-eight - had been released from a British hospital after he´d had a kidney stone removed. He saluted his fans by announcing, "I'm back on the field, thirsty for new goals in life."

The driver interrupted my pop culture reverie. "Because we were Portuguese, they always asked us for money, medicines and such. I said, 'No, I cannot.' One Friday there was a celebration in the village. It was a cousin's birthday party, or something. Pelé went there with his aunt. On Sunday I drove there to pick him up. As I drove into the village, I could see something in the road. As I got closer, I could see it was a body. It was the body of a child. They had cut off its head - you know, cut it off like a chicken. It was Pelé. They cut the head off, and they cut off the legs. And the arms were cut, also. They laid the pieces out in order, the head, the arms, the legs - all in order. They cut them. They knew I was going there to pick him up, and they laid him out on the road so that I could see him."

The driver turned to the outside where the cold rain and twisting tree were now a solace. He turned back, and said, "So, I agreed. I agreed to teach the soldiers. I told no one. It took me fourteen months."

I was light-headed. I'd eaten nothing since lunch, and now it was after nine. The driver continued,

"I went there with two of my men. I found the man who did that to Pelé. And, I killed him." After a hesitation, perhaps considering the effect this information had on me, the driver added, "His own men were afraid of him. He was the Devil." *Yes, yes, of course,* I nodded.

I wanted nothing more than to go into my house, eat something, and play with my fluffy, new towels. But it is not every day that I find myself in the company of a killer wishing to talk about his experience, and sending him off at this point in his story on such a miserable night seemed inhuman. "Would you like to come in for a glass of wine or a cup of tea?" I asked.

The driver agreed immediately. He unfolded himself and came around to my side of the car, and stood courteously in the rain as I handed him first the umbrella, and then the bags one by one until I could free myself. We entered the gate, and walked up the steps. We stopped in my dining room to drop off the packages before continuing into my kitchen. Anyone noticing his slight, side-ward limp would assume it was normal stiffness from a day spent driving. He perched on the edge of my small bistro chair like a bird that might fly off any second.

I lunged for the bottle of red wine on the counter. The driver accepted the glass I set before him, but stopped me from pouring at two fingers, saying he had another 45 minutes to drive that night. He was only driving that night because one of his young employees had called in sick. He had picked me up in a black Peugeot 508 wagon. He still works as an engineer. The cars are a second business.

I was starving. I moved economically around the kitchen, sliding on the granite floor in my socks. I was afraid to make sudden movements. I asked him small questions as I pulled rye crackers, and a jar of pimentos from the cupboard. To avoid jangling silverware in the drawer, I slid scissors from the Ahmad's tea tin on the counter. Inside the refrigerator door I found a package of pre-sliced white cheese. The pimento jar lid came off easily with just a soft *thwuck*, but the peppers were whole, and so tightly packed I panicked before just using my fingers. I pryed out the dripping, red skirts, and ripped them into jagged slivers, laying them on the cheese I cut smaller with scissors to fit the dark slabs. I laid the canapes before the driver. He looked pleased, but he said, "I hope that is not for me. I don't eat. Well, I eat like a bird. But I will drink with you."

I sat down across from him and picked up the first cracker. It took all of my willpower to nibble, and not shove the cracker into my mouth, and finish it two bites. "I am split down the middle," said the driver. "I like literature and music. Every kind of music. I like jazz. I like John Coltrane. I like Miles Davis." He paused after each name. It was as if confessing to successively worse crimes, waiting for my reaction before continuing. I took bigger bites.

I had listened to jazz almost exclusively in the 1980s. There was a great local band with a sax player named "Smokey Joe Pantucci" that played Herbie Hancock, and The Jazz Crusaders. I went to see them almost every week. My friend, Ginger Jones had given me a cassette tape that she'd made from her vinyl of drummer, Jack DeJohnette. I'd gone to see DeJohnette in Amarante, Portugal at the MIMO Festival just the past summer. The driver had not known about this nearby concert, but he did know DeJohnette's music and he agreed this American is an international treasure. We reminisced about other jazz artists of the period we both liked; Brazilian singer, Flora Purim, American trumpeter Don Cherry. At some point, inspired by a tub of miso on my counter I leapt up and sang the sparse lyric of Cherry's "Brown Rice," before settling down to another cracker.

I mentioned hitchhiking with a friend to see pianist Barry Harris with Wayne Shorter at Chicago's Jazz Showcase, and the Hampton

Hawes Trio recording with Leroy Vinnegar that I have. He knew all of these guys. He even knew the great contemporary Cuban piano player, Alfredo Rodriguez who I'd only recently discovered at the Montreaux Jazz Festival. When the driver said he wanted to go outside for his electronic cigarettes I kept him inside by pulling out a plastic bag of cigarettes I sometimes have in the back of my freezer. We stood just outside on the sheltered balcony blowing smoke out into the rain as the cool air seeped in around us. The driver told me his father had just died one month earlier.

"My father never once touched me," he said. (Later I learned about this.) "When we would meet on the street he spoke to me formally, 'Good day, Mr (redacted) and I would reply, 'Good day, Mr (redacted)'" The driver told me his own now-grown son tries to trick him into hugs. "But I never hug anyone." Reaching his arms forward like Frankenstein's monster he stepped toward me, and tapped so quickly and so lightly behind my shoulders that it could not really be said to have happened at all. "The most I can do is like this," he said. He stepped back and the air in the kitchen seemed to warm with his relief that it was over.

I was tired now, and wanted to see him off. Enough had been said I thought. We walked back through the dining room. At my table the driver froze. "If you share this story, just say it was from 'some guy,'" he said. *OK*, I said. Suddenly, he blurted out his full name, and eyeing a notebook on my dining room table he asked for a piece of paper. The pen was already in his hand. I folded the book open to a blank page, handed it to him, and he wrote out his full name in that flowery, Old-World script that I can´t read. It looks purely decorative. As I was marvelling that anyone could read the curlicues, he asked if I would like to see his Citizen's Card. Before I could stammer that this wasn't necessary at all, he was holding a milky, laminated plastic card with a fingernail-sized photo of himself close to my eyes. I pretended to scrutinize his details while willing myself to see nothing beyond the iridescent, tamper-proof plastic.

We walked to the front door, shook hands. I stood waving cheerily from my porch as the driver closed the gate, checked the latch twice to make sure it was secure, got into his car and drove away. Inside the kitchen I ate the last cracker. I'd finally eaten all four. Clearing the dishes, I noticed the sip he´d left in his glass, like a drop of blood. Like something left for someone who could not be with us that night.

The Angolan War had not made sense to me. I finished high school, entered college, dropped out of college, started a business, went back to college, began work as a journalist, and hosted sleepovers for my daughter's little friends all to a backdrop of black men in bandoliers killing each other in faraway jungles. Occasionally I´d glance up at the TV from homework, then from frosting cupcakes for the school bake sale when the *rat-tat-tat* of gunfire broke my concentration, but only occasionally. Mainly it was like an exotic-themed wallpaper. Exciting at first, it had grown faded and curled up at the edges.

Trying to catch up now with what I'd missed during all those years left me only more confused. The US had joined South Africa's Apartheid government to back a Communist warlord trained in Red China under Chairman Mao to overthrow a democratically-elected physician and poet. The US-backed UNITA soldiers had enslaved 10,000 children, documented by Human Rights Watch. US taxpayers had tossed hundreds of millions of dollars in "kickbacks" alone to these same guerrillas, who journalists reported for a decade terrorizing their people before the US slunk away after the Communist warlord died in 2002. Half a million people were dead. Many millions more were left shattered and displaced. When one UNITA guerrilla was miffed that a Portuguese engineer refused to give him kickbacks, he murdered the child Pelé out of spite.

I also had not understood why President Reagan praised rampaging foreign blacks as "freedom fighters" while at the same time he mocked everyday black citizens at home as "Welfare Queens." Isn´t welfare for others the foundation that all great world religions, and civil society itself are built upon? Next President, Bill Clinton signed the *Violent Crime Control and Law Enforcement Act* as his blue-eyed soccer-mom wife Hilary cheered because black men were "Super Predators," best locked up, or shot with the prisons and military hardware provided to neighborhood police departments under the bill. Senator Joe Biden wrote that bill. He bragged his bill would do "everything but hang people for jaywalking." While invoking *nostalgia for lynching* the US government was showering money on black psychopaths in Portugal´s former African colonies.

In 2016 Muhiyidin d`Baha, the soft-spoken Bahá'í most associated with the Black Lives Matter movement, (although he also worked on Green Party organizing, public education and community gardening,) explained that the prisons were built to warehouse people whose jobs Reagan and Clinton had sent away under foreign trade agreements including NAFTA (the North American Free Trade Agreement.) Today domestic US prisons lockup 25% of the world´s prisoners although the US population is only 3%.

More and more reasons are invented to take people´s freedom, including that of people who cannot pay parking tickets, parents who cannot pay their children´s school lunch bills, and peaceful protestors who are supposed to be protected under Constitutional rights of free speech and congregation. Even US children are imprisoned. As California Attorney General, Vice President Kamala Harris, whose state prison system locked up children as young as 14 with adults tweeted proudly, "Today, more than

2,000 volunteer inmate firefighters, *including 58 youth offenders*, are battling wildfire flames throughout CA… (#CarrFire #FergusonFire #MendocinoComplex. @CACorrections" August 1, 2018), my italics. Even child labour laws are ignored to provide free labour for hazardous jobs and to rent out to corporations paying pennies on the legal minimum wage.

Two hundred years after the Irish General Wellesley declared there are no winners in war, the American General Eisenhower wrote, "The consequences of allowing the military-industrial complex to wage war, exhaust our resources and dictate our national priorities are beyond grave: Every gun that is made, every warship launched, every rocket fired signifies, in the final sense, a theft from those who hunger and are not fed, those who are cold and are not clothed. This world in arms is not spending money alone. It is spending the sweat of its laborers, the genius of its scientists, the hopes of its children. The cost of one modern heavy bomber is this: a modern brick school in more than 30 cities. It is two electric power plants, each serving a town of 60,000 population. It is two fine, fully equipped hospitals. It is some fifty miles of concrete pavement. We pay for a single fighter plane with a half million bushels of wheat. We pay for a single destroyer with new homes that could have housed more than 8,000 people…This is not a way of life at all, in any true sense. Under the cloud of threatening war, it is humanity hanging from a cross of iron."

This was part of the outgoing US President Eisenhower´s 1953 speech to the American Society of Newspaper Editors. When I posted his speech on Facebook/Meta in May 2022, the speech was immediately torn down, and my Facebook account was "Restricted for Violating Community Standards." At a time when hundreds of journalists have been fired, censored, demonized, imprisoned, and tortured inside the US and in other sovereign nations for publishing US war crimes and criminal activities of the pharmaceutical industry, remembering history has become "against community standards." Not in my community!

From my new home in Portugal, I watched hurricanes, floods and fires of Biblical proportions ravage my country. I watched monthly mass shootings become twice-monthly, then twice-weekly, and an opioid crisis created by the pharmaceutical industry cripple entire regions with death and despair. I watched tens of millions of Americans become jobless, then homeless as a health crisis created in a private lab funded by US tax dollars swept a country with no healthcare. I watched 2,000 worker strikes be ignored by the mainstream media, and I participated in another Presidential Election in which all of the candidates I agreed with were barred from debates, and from media coverage. (Green Party candidate Dr. Jill Stein was sued for even running a campaign.) And, I was stunned when the only thing the two US political parties could agree on before going on Christmas vacations was to give the military industrial complex another Trillion dollars. President "hang people for jaywalking" Joe's first acts in office were 1) Bomb Syria, 2) Bomb Somalia, and 3) Bomb Iran.

A Portuguese friend working teaching English on US military bases - yes, you read that right, literacy is down after systematic defunding of education to pay for wars and public giveaways to private corporations - was amazed how often his US soldier students told him they joined the military "to get my teeth fixed." The US minimum wage has been frozen since 2001 at just $7.25 an hour. The US median annual income of $36,000 will not buy even one year at an American university.

In 2009 the year after Barack Obama was elected President on a campaign of Hope, Harvard University published a study finding that 45,000 US citizens die every year in the US because the country has no public healthcare. A decade after the "Affordable Care Act," written by and for the private insurance industry to block efforts at establishing public healthcare, a 2020 Yale University study found the number of Americans dying needlessly each year because the US has no public healthcare had climbed to 70,000. For the past 50 years US national priorities are catalogued in policies tailor-made to create armies of citizens so desperate that they are willing to waste themselves in foreign wars rather than die on US streets with periodontal disease, or be imprisoned and used as slave labour.

I met other veterans in Charleston, South Carolina between 2014 and 2017 when volunteering with the homeless (as had Muhiyidin.) Under the I-26 overpass 125 people lived in muddy tents, where they were served by professional and volunteer social workers, until April 2016 when the liberal mayor John Tecklenberg "liberated" the camp, scattering residents to parts unknown, and destroying their meager belongings, moving in his SWAT team when I was in meetings at the White House and in the Capitol Building with State Representative Wendell Gilliard and other activists to present our research and best-practice solution to our state's growing homelessness. (I prepared a legal structure for a tiny house village.)

One of the camp occupants was a fulltime employee of Boeing, the world's second largest weapons contractor. Although flush with $93 Million from fleecing South Carolinians just its first year in the state, and haemorrhaging profits, the weapons contractor would not pay its employee enough to afford housing for himself and his family back in Washington State. I visited Devohn one night at the camp to find him huddled with a group of men around dinner of half-cooked, bloody turtle pulled from the Ashley River. (Devohn was one of the camp residents I brought to meet White House Deputy Assistant for Intergovernmental Affairs, Jerry Abrams, and Housing and Urban Development staff.)

Other veterans I met around this time were luckier. These were elite veterans of wars with pretty, paint color-sounding names; *New Dawn*, and *Desert Storm*. When I knocked on the door of my neighbor's suburban home, and the handsome Mexican-American who answered explained that my neighbor was visiting her grandkids, and had leased her home to his company for a few months while they worked near North Charleston's military bases, and invited me in, I accepted. Inside were his colleagues. All were exceptionally good looking, and personable. They ranged in age from 24-58 and were nursing beers and old injuries after a long week of selling mercenary work to other veterans. They still wore uniforms - putty-colored polo shirts with the logo of their Northern Virginia employer embroidered over their hearts.

The hunkiest of the bunch, a 38-year-old ex-Navy SEAL who could model for *Men's Health*, or any body-building magazine (and, I'd even pick it up and thumb through it if waiting in line at the checkout stand) was rubbing his knees, wincing in pain. I expressed surprise, *You look so fit!* He began listing his injuries; a broken back, a broken neck, multiple knee and arm surgeries…. My eyes widened. His fresh-faced, 26-year-old colleague broke in, "We *all* have these injuries! It comes from carrying two hundred pounds of equipment on our backs. The human body is not built to withstand this abuse!"

Here were the cream of elite US veterans, and all were as broken as the one-legged birds that my cat Dinky used to drag through the cat door. I dated the handsome Mexican-American man a few times before he returned to Northern Virginia. Then he Skyped me, showing me his truck, his modest town home, and his offices, where he introduced me to more of his work colleagues. I had to break it off, explaining my upcoming move to Portugal. As little direct experience as I´d had with the US military, I´d had more than enough.

I met the driver again a few months later at an old marina in Porto, not far from where he grew up in Gondomar. It was still raining. In the daylight filtered through a faded cloth awning his eyes sparkled like Coca Cola with melting ice. He said that he is writing a book of stories patterned after Ágota Kristóf's *Trilogy of the City of K*, a story of twin brothers torn apart by World War II. His story - the story that inspired this one - is called "K." The driver was sent to live with an aunt for his safety after his younger brother died from an illness, driving his mother mad with grief. The aunt was an educated woman. She introduced him to music and literature. During his two-year Portuguese military service the driver was stationed in a library, where he continued to nurture his intellect with wider reading.

Another chapter in the driver's book is *Jacinto*. Jacinto was a man who did odd jobs around his father's jewelry factory. Taunted by the other workers for being "special," Jacinto one day got fed up and threw an iron bar at his abusers. He was fired. He became homeless. But despite sleeping in abandoned sheds, and going hungry, Jacinto was too proud to accept handouts. So, the driver developed a plan. He began visiting the areas Jacinto stayed, pretending to run into Jacinto by accident. He´d strike up conversation, then ask his old friend to walk with him so they could continue their conversation. Soon, they would arrive outside a café, where the driver would realize that he was hungry, and ask Jacinto to accompany him inside, so that he did not have to eat alone. Jacinto passed away many years ago, but the driver uses this technique today around Porto where people are hungry, and too proud to accept handouts. Cigarettes are sometimes involved as tokens of shared experience.

In Angola, the driver received a citizen card with a false Cuban identity. The name on that card read *Rodolfo Ardillez*. Captain Ardillez received a *Medalha de Merito militar - 1° Classe* for his actions in the province of Uíge and in the battle of Cuito

Canavale. It was presented by the Angolan General Pitra Petroff, and the Cuban General Cintra Frias. In Angola he associated with Angolan General France N'dalu , Major Higino Carneiro, Major "Quick Pass," and Russian military personnel. Survivors of the 30 year conflict today - from both sides - share memories and observations in an online chat room. The driver´s leg was blown off after he returned to his public life, when he stepped on a forgotten landmine at an engineering site.

In 1986 I was the Promotion Director for KHCC-FM, Kansas Public Radio. I supported my student husband on my salary of $18,000 a year. The "Tax Reform Act of 1986" lowered the top tax rate from 50% to 28%, and raised the bottom tax rate from 11% to 15% - the first time in US income tax history that the top tax rate was lowered, and the bottom rate was increased at the same time. I modelled myself a professional woman like Melanie Griffith a few years later in *Working Girls* as far as my budget allowed. I bought an expensive Japanese wool twill trench coat that year at the most exclusive shop in Hutchinson, Kansas. In 2017 when I gave the coat away it looked brand new.

I wonder how much of my taxes went to buy that land mine that blew off the secret soldier's leg? If I hadn´t paid for bombs and kickbacks, might I might still have a cashmere sweater or pussy-bow silk blouse from that era of quality? I know I would have bought more books, and be better read today. This story might even have been easier to write, and better written. Instead, I wound up with a new, one-legged friend. Born in a country where healthcare, education and human dignity are all basic rights, he returned. Born in a country Hell-bent on crippling the world, I left. We don´t agree on everything, but we do share many things. Chief among them is gratitude.

I Brined A Turkey

Bacalhau is salted codfish. It´s traditionally eaten here at Christmas - and at too many other times. When I eat *bacalhau* what happens is that I either choke on a bone, or must pretend to choke on a bone so that the gagging and expectoration that follow seem reasonable. Most people who eat *bacalhau* anywhere near me never again consider it a festive dish.

Bacalhau enthusiasts will insist that everyone within range <u>who did not order the dish</u> "Try some!" You might consider these to be generous people. I consider them to be like the bad cats with an uncanny ability to target the one person in the room who is terrified of cats, or who is allergic to cats, or who just hates cats, and jump on their lap and torment them. *Bacalhau* eaters are worse than cats though, because one cannot smack them away, at least not in a public place like a restaurant. *Bacalhau* eaters count on this, of course. Sometimes smiling broadly and saying, "I love *bacalhau*, but I had it already for lunch today!" (or breakfast, if necessary,) will be enough to be left in peace. The performance is critical, however. "Lucky you!" is the response you are looking for, with the cod-eaters diving into their unappetizing grey slab, and leaving you alone. A lackluster performance may be mistaken for politeness, which they will outmaneuver with more politeness, and continued fork jabbing in your direction. An unnaturally intense, almost manic delight at the very word is required on your part to be free.

Believe you me, not accepting the *bacalhau* is the only polite response from me! No one who succeeds asks me twice. I respect the *bacalhau* culture, the fishermen, their hardships, the history, the reliability of the stuff as a protein source to keep people alive. But I respect my mouth's reliability as a spoilage detection and ejection system before I am poisoned even more. My advice whenever *bacalhau* threatens your vicinity is to locate plenty of napkins, preferably the disposable kind.

So, this Christmas I decided to invite a few friends for a traditional American-style dinner featuring roast turkey. My relationship with poultry has also been strained. The meat served in my house growing up was of such low quality, and so haphazardly prepared that I did my best to avoid it. My mother bought only the cheapest cuts of meat, and only when past their expiration dates. Usually, she was completely drunk when she prepared them. I preferred anaemia.

On the other hand, my mother was turned-on by meat. She loved it! To anyone who would listen she bragged that she preferred her meat so rare as to be "bloody." One restaurant waiter (who had probably heard her histrionics one time too many,) obeyed her instructions. Watching my mother choke down a cold, bloody hamburger between successive refills of Scotch ranks low on the scale of childhood traumas, but it must rank on there somewhere.

From my parents' home I moved into a Midwestern college dormitory, and paid my tuition by working in the school cafeteria under the Work-Study Program. (This was in the 1970s when such a thing was possible.) I soon learned that "chicken-fried steaks," which were popular in the area were not poultry, but bloody beef masquerading as chicken. During the two years I lived in that oxblood brick dormitory I must have eaten some meat, but the only foods I recall with any clarity were the cafeteria's "Bavarian cream," a concoction of fruit-flavored gelatin mixed with whipped cream, and hominy grits, which were corn kernels swollen for reasons unknown in a lye bath until all flavor was removed, and they resembled giant, cartoon teeth. I also became a cole slaw aficiando during my cafeteria tenure, because my boss, the dining room manager, taught me to make it in a distinctive way. He stood over me instructing me to slam the head onto the counter again and again until its cone-shaped core lifted out easily. "Harder!" he would yell, "Again! Harder!" Like an army drill sergeant, he demanded I perfect his technique. I arrived at the campus very thin, and in a state of anaemia. The dining room manager was also pale and thin, with watery blue eyes. He seemed delicate for a man. I suspect that he was trying to help toughen me up in kinship, and that this was as close to a martial arts lesson as his job description would allow. (It is also as far as I ever progressed in the martial arts.)

Soon after moving out of the dormitory, I fell in with a group of vegetarians. This group I merged with naturally as I never quite had with my Gamma Sigma Sigma sorority sisters. Soon I became a *professional vegetarian* when I was hired for a manager position in a vegetarian co-

I BRINED A TURKEY

operative, the 2,500-member Columbia Community Grocery.

These were the times, and this was the place where meetings called to discuss the ethical questions about selling pet food made with animal products in a vegetarian coop drew sizable crowds, and the passionate debates went on for hours without name-calling, or "partisan" rancor. When the town's vegetarian, Paquin Street Café restaurant closed (because the commune where most of its workers lived disbanded,) my friends, Randy, Renie, Jim and I opened The Catalpa Tree Café. I wrote a book about vegetarian foods. Only thrice in 10 years did I succumb to temptations of the flesh. Once Frank Fillo's game of peek-a-boo with his grandmother's left- over Thanksgiving turkey became too much for me to ignore. Perhaps he was hypnotizing me with the movement of the shiny aluminum foil. The wheedling badgering, and the wiggling of a flaccid strip of turkey with a dangling bit of golden roasted skin in front of my mouth wore me down until I bit. "Um, delicious," I said. (It really was).

The second time was when I ate a can of tuna fish, but immediately after I wrote an elegy for the fish, so this time may not count. The third time was when I was working on a radio series, "Missouri Folklore," and reporting on an annual Mens BBQ 'Coon Supper that had occurred on the same day during the Christmas holidays for 100 years at a tiny rural church. I observed the meal's preparations, (which I'd rather not go into right now,) and I was offered a sample. Boiled, defatted, smoked for hours, then re-cooked in tomato-based barbecue sauce it could have been anything - an innocent piece of eggplant. Then, one old coon hunter - his eyes glinting ghoulishly - told me that when *treed*, which means cornered in a tree with no chance of escape, the racoons cry. "They sound just like a kitty cat," he said. He had to add that "They are close cousins." I declined their invitation to be the sole female guest of honor at the dinner-

I BRINED A TURKEY

probably more likely the entertainment, as they watched me eat a whole raccoon - because, alas, I was under deadline and urgently needed back at the studio.

Until my late thirties buying meat was confined to one year when I was in seventh grade. Alice Imler and I walked home from middle school through the downtown business center. Somehow we discovered that our best snack value was hanging on a string in the Italian butcher shop. It cost less than a candy bar to buy the two, connected pepperoni sausages that the butcher snipped into two for us. Most days we had enough extra coins to buy a loaf of Italian bread at the bakery nearby. In those days no one except mountain climbers used backpacks. We carried our canvas-bound textbooks. Here they served as bistro tables, which we held level in front of us to slide the white paper bag of bread back and forth between us. Clutching our pepperonis, chomping and schlepping our way up Green Village Road we felt very cosmopolitan. We were two little, weird, long-haired girls enjoying life to the fullest.

In 1978 I became a vegetarian. This was easy because most of us lived on beans and rice at this stage in our lives. We cooked simply. We did not eat out. Only after moving to South Carolina, the land where Southern fried chicken and pork barbecue collide did I add some meat back into my diet. In 1990 in Charleston vegetarianism was such an outlandish concept that whenever conversation lulled, I was called upon to defend my diet. One mother in the playgroup took pity on me, and referred me to a church she accidentally attended one time where she suspected other vegetarians might be lurking. I joined. Then, in 1999 my eight-year old daughter announced that she was becoming a vegetarian after she watched an afternoon talk show that exposed unsavory parts of the meat industry.

Until she went away to college, again I had little contact with meat. During her college years, mostly it was that I was smacked in the face with it. She went to school in New York City, and lived in a dormitory on the edge of Chinatown. Whenever I visited I insisted she take me to buy the exotic things that did not exist in South Carolina. My daughter despised Chinatown, and imposed very strict time limits for my shopping. She stood outside on the sidewalk, a scarf wrapped around her mouth and nose to shield her from the odor of death all around. She jostled the crowds on the small sidewalks to avoid being pushed any closer to the pails of fish entrails, eels, and gaping pig's heads, making it clear that if I was not out fast, she'd leave me there and I'd have to find my way back to her dorm alone. I lived in a small town and had no sense of the city. So, she'd set her watch. I'd rush into the shops ducking between dried ducks and hams hanging from low ceilings and low doorways. If my daughter was still outside, (and kept her complaints at least civil,) I shared with her the treats of sandalwood *Bee and Flower* soap, knobs of bitter ginseng, beautiful tiny jars of

Tiger Balm, and liquorice-infused, salted dried plums.

Today when I order meat in restaurants, which is almost the only time I eat it, my instructions to the waiters are exactly the opposite of my mother's. *Cooked brown—all the way through. Dried out. No pink or wetness. It can even be a little burnt,* I say. When the plate arrives, I have napkins already balled anxiously in my fists. I inspect the meat carefully. Half the time I slide the plate away, and ask for it to be cooked more. Sometimes I just cover it with a napkin and ask for the bill. So, I took nothing for granted about buying and cooking a fresh turkey for 19 guests a few days before Christmas.

A former professional butcher from a cattle-rearing part of the US, who owns a wine and tour business in Porto recommended the best butcher. This meat expert told me this butcher shop supplies meat to Porto's finest restaurants. He enthused that the animals were *personally known,* and *aged on the premises.* However, just how close the butchers really are to the animals is probably open to interpretation. Do they act as genial uncles—creepy uncles—stopping in periodically with advice? ("Eat up!") I imagined the carefree youngster animals frolicking through their childhood and teen years, ogling the chickens, and teasing the cows as turkeys will, until that fateful day the genial uncle arrives with *the serious talk.* This particular *talho* is not far from where I lived for a few months in Matosinhos, home of the "World's Best Seafood." I knew it as a location at the crossroads of stampeding ironies.

Although I´ve had limited contact with actual meat, the Portuguese word for butcher shop was one of the first I picked up. That´s because one passes so many butcher shops in Portugal, and like "Baby's First Words" picture books, each shop has a display window showing the products under the word, *talho.* Also, "Tally ho!" is an expression associated with horseback hunting. I picture deer hunts, and hare hunts, Norsemen swooping across Europe clubbing everything in their paths, and my mother Nancy clubbing baby calves to slaver over their still-warm bodies served on a bone china plate.

Across the street from the recommended *talho* is a Burger King with a giant, ersatz street art of a portly, tattooed Portuguese male in baggy shorts, ball cap, and hipster sneakers swallowing a whole, uncooked fish. The Burger King corporate logo is next to his sneakered feet. This is just a few blocks from the town's famous Rua Heróis de França seafood restaurants where diners may sit inches from passing cars as the grill-masters cook over hot charcoal grills, sometimes singing to passersby.

Burger King sells no fish in Portugal. Not whole, not raw, fileted or fried, and while the artist has taken pains to create a hip, modern-day, *ze povinho*, Burger King has been certified by the Union of Concerned Scientists as the least hip restaurant on the planet, far below Wendy's and McDonald's, citing its grotesque human rights violations, and crediting Burger King with the destruction of half of Brazil's indigenous savanna. "Have it your way," is the company's motto - unless your way is fish, human rights, biodiversity, or breathing oxygen. At least I knew where the *talho* was.

All I had to do now was to spend an afternoon watching YouTube cooking videos. After playing Whac-A-Mole with all the advertising pop-ups, I was exhausted, but I believed I had learned enough to cook a turkey. From my new community of carnivore friends I had learned the secret to tender, succulent meat is *brining* the turkey. This means soaking the turkey in salt water, something which seemed counter-indicative to me, as salt draws out moisture. The most important thing is I learned was that to avoid poisoning guests, one should brine the turkey inside the refrigerator. This prevents bacterial growth. It also prevents the injuries associated with falling downstairs while carrying the carcass up to the bathtub to soak, slipping on the blood trail.

In preparation I pulled out the refrigerator vegetable bin. To get the refrigerator door open wide enough to pull out the bin, I had to move the refrigerator as far from the wall as the short cord would allow. This blocked half of the entrance door into the kitchen. As I was dieting anyway in anticipation of the feast, I simply sucked in my stomach and squeezed in and out through the opening. From the American National Turkey Federation website, under "Turkey 101" I learned, "If you want plenty of leftovers, plan for 1.25 to 1.5 pounds per person." Not wanting the reputation of a stingy hostess, I accepted this advice, and converted the twenty-eight-pound American turkey required for 19 guests into one 13-kilogram Portuguese turkey.

Ten days before the dinner I went to the *talho* to inspect it. I was impressed by its parking lot,

I BRINED A TURKEY

which was remarkably free of trash considering its proximity to the fast-food neighbor. Entering the shop I found it odorless, and free of pests. I was greeted by a gentleman with luxurious snowy-white hair wearing a spotless white lab coat like a doctor. He assured me that he would have no problem getting me a 12-13 kilogram turkey on three days' notice, quoted me a price of "about 3.90 per kilogram." He refused a deposit, and told me to pick up the turkey Saturday afternoon. My dinner was on Monday. I calculated that I needed 12 hours to brine the bird, six hours to cook it, 30 minutes to let it "rest."

During the week I passed many *talhos* advertising fresh turkey for much less per kilogram, but I consoled myself with the knowledge that I was working with a distinguished *doctor-butcher* whose carcasses had been *personally known*. Perhaps they'd been given a balanced diet including vegetables. Perhaps even educated in some way? Whenever I doubted my decision to buy the turkey from this famous *talho* I replaced doubt with images of a story-book farm where I imagined this *talho's* animals all lived. Here the animals frolicked freely. The chickens clucked in kaffeeklatsches, the teenaged turkeys misbehaved, and the baleful, doe-eyed cows stood apart like bashful wallflowers at a dance. Because I always think of the worst scenario, I also imagined the *serious talk*. It went something like this, "*Now, João. You've had a very nice life at this quintel. Plenty to eat, squishy mud beneath your feet. It's time to grow up. Face the facts of life. Yours ends today.*" I was sure though that this conversation would be handled very professionally, or else this *talho* would never maintain its fine reputation.

On Saturday morning I headed to the *feira* near my house early in the morning. On a good day two hundred vendors show up at the *Senhora da Hora Feira*. Most drive in from regional manufacturing and agricultural areas in white panel vans with their seats removed to stack the goods from the floor to the headliners. Vendors

I BRINED A TURKEY

lay their goods out on tables, and hang them from ropes. Most have plastic tarps over themselves and their goods as relief from the sun and the rain because *feiras* are outside with no shelter.

Today was not a good day. There was no sun, and plenty of rain. My friend, Norma who is a wonderful cook and hostess whose mojo I'd hoped would rub off on me, cancelled on the flimsy excuse that 50-kilometer-per-hour winds and heavy rain would cancel the *feira*. The *feira* was packed to capacity. Wind pelted rain on a slant, making umbrellas as superfluous as sticks. Since I don´t have an umbrella, ever since my hairdresser´s umbrella broke, I pulled the hood of my raincoat farther over my face, and walked faster.

The *feiras* of Portugal are one of my favorite places. They sell everything and anything one could possibly want to buy. Everyone is friendly, so if you are looking for something in particular, you can just ask anyone for directions. Woolen socks, toe nail clippers, cotton pajamas, leather clogs, spools of thread and decorative trims, real linen bedsheets, high-quality cottons, underwear, knockoff colognes, hand-forged steel pitchforks, fresh-caught fish, still-alive chickens, rabbits, and songbirds in citrus-colors, soft cheeses, smoked dried meats, fresh flowers, fruits and vegetables, French and German luxury brand fashions, and fabrics made in Portugal for Burberry, Tommy Hilfiger, and Marimekko are all sold at larger *feiras* at reasonable prices. That day my shopping list included more of the locally-made, ergonomic, wood-handled cutlery, broccoli and cauliflower I planned to mound up like Christmas trees on platters of recycled Spanish green glass, parsley, which vendors give away for free, and bunches of white *margarida* flowers to spread cheer throughout my rather dark house.

Each of the vendors has a designated *stick person*. This is a person with a stick who periodically pokes the "*Vs*" in the tarps that form in rainy

I BRINED A TURKEY

weather before they get too full and heavy and fall down or otherwise drench the goods. I was darting between the vendor rows, and watching my feet to avoid tripping on a guy-wire or tarp pole, and hit my head on a full "*V*," sending a bucketful of icy water showering down my neck and sweater inside the rain poncho. As I stumbled out into the main throughfare, a woman shrugged and smiled at me. I smiled back. The wind would have me dry in no time. Everyone seemed to be smiling with the camaraderie of lunatics.

The red awning of the food truck beckoned with its balmy luxury of a plastic walled courtyard, its comfortable chairs, and its tables and napkin dispensers. This business is operated by a family of twin sisters, and the glowering husband of one. I've never figured out whose. It has a TV set to show Portuguese sports, and an L-shaped, glass-fronted counter that is stocked with homemade omelets, breaded pork cutlets, squid and parsley salad, and *rabanadas*. Its printed menu is larger than in most brick and mortar cafes, and everything they make is good. Given my complicated relationship with meat, it may come as a surprise that I usually start my *feira* mornings by stopping off here to get one of the *bifanas* along with an *abatanado*. Today I added a bowl of soup, a broth thickened with potatoes, with tender shredded carrot and cabbage morsels, and sat back watching the linens vendor across the aisle. She dresses like an indie-rock musician and reminds me of Carrie Brownstein in tall boots and slim jeans, but with zany Portuguese hair.

Today she is negotiating the sale of a holiday tablecloth with a customer and they both ignore the white tablecloth with a holly leaf border flapping violently in the wind a few feet from their heads. The wind finally wins, ripping down the cloth. This may have settled the sale with sympathy, because the customer quickly agrees to the price, leaves clutching her wrapped package, and the vendor comes around her tables to pick up her cloth from the ground. The end of

I BRINED A TURKEY

the performance signals my time to leave the sanctuary.

I visited the vegetable vendors first, grabbing handfuls of plump, broad green beans, sweet, fist-sized Portuguese broccoli and cauliflower cradled in long leaves, which I use in tofu stir-fries, and tightening my billowing rain hood, marched diagonally across the boulevard. Passing the chirping windup toys, the jewelry vendors, rug and curtain vendors I arrived at the cutlery and basket vendor. She disappeared into her van, returning with knives, but no forks, so I bought her knives, making a mental note to look elsewhere for forks. It was time to return to the white-haired doctor-butcher, so I called a ride share.

The ride-share driver was a lovely man named Fernando with the tweedy bearing of a retired university professor. He spoke a beautiful and formal English. When I told him that I was going to the butcher shop that a *professional gourmet* had raved about, he asked if he might join me. I was delighted to have his moral support, and possibly his help carrying a thirteen-kilogram turkey. We dropped my *feira* haul off at my house on the way, where I also picked up my oven's enamelled drip pan so I could make sure the turkey I bought would fit in my oven. Outside the *talho* door was a cluster of waiting people. Fernando, a large and imposing man, pushed past them. Inside, a lively throng of about ten more customers waited. Fernando marched to the rear of the shop with me following. He hailed a wiry young butcher carrying a whole baby pig, *leitão*, gave my name and my order, and the butcher disappeared through a rear door, leaving Fernando to translate the disappointing news that the shop had only a *ten-kilogram turkey* for me.

Great, I thought. My guests would leave hungry, and I´d be forever known around Porto as a stingy hostess. I was muttering in irritation when the butcher reappeared holding a bruised-looking bird. He spread out its wings, wiggled them and grinned, cruelly, I thought, mocking its inability to fly. I said it was *OK* before he added insult to injury and dropped the poor thing on the floor. We trooped into the glassed-in booth where the baby pig was removed, and I set my oven's drip pan on the slab. The turkey fit with no room to spare. Fernando asked if I wanted the butcher to clean the turkey. *Yes, of course,* I said, for 3.90 a kilo, I expected it clean. The butcher grinned down at white stubs poking up from the skin, haphazardly yanked out one or two then stretched the turkey's neck out to its full extension, and asked where I wanted it chopped. I looked away. Fernando decided. He carried the bird in a thick plastic bag the butcher put it in, inside the drip pan.

A tiny, rouged and powdered creature wearing Coke-bottle eyeglasses, and a leopard-print coat with a sheer, chiffon scarf tied around her neck sat at the cash register. She was so short her head was level with the cash drawer. She had to stretch her neck out to its full extension to peer under her eyeglasses and over the edge of the drawer each time she made change for a customer. The white-haired doctor-butcher appeared next to her to give me the total cost. I paid, and gallant Fernando carried the bird in its pan, put it in the trunk of his car, and at my house, insisted on carrying it into the kitchen for me. We exchanged it at the kitchen doorway, which he could not get through now blocked as it was by the refrigerator. We wished each other a pleasant Christmas, and I followed him back outside and all the way to his car, delaying the inevitable moment when I´d be left alone with the turkey.

In the bright light of my kitchen window in the bright white porcelain sink were - feathers! White stubs of feathers covered my turkey! Quills sized to write sonnets! Pin feathers to stuff pillows! All over my "cleaned" turkey! I squeezed back through the door to get my bathroom tweezers and began plucking. Each time I pulled a feather

I BRINED A TURKEY

from of the limp, yellowish-pinkish-purplish skin I heard a sound like a foot being pulled out of mud. Each sucking sound was barely audible, but my head was close enough to see each feather, so each tiny sound was heard distinctly.

I must have pulled sixty feathers. I had plenty of time to think. Are feathers a status symbol, indicating the bird is from a "noble butcher" who *knows his animals*, or had they treated me shabbily because of my obvious inexperience buying a fresh turkey? Was meanness a side effect of consuming large quantities of meat? Do tribes of carnivores typically behave this way when facing near-vegetarians? Suddenly, a pride for US poultry workers swelled in my breast. Who would have guessed that these most abused, and underpaid of all abused and underpaid US workers, toiling in gothic-horror conditions, do a far superior job of cleaning poultry than Europe's top *talho*. On another continent another immigrant had proof. After 20 minutes of plucking, listening, rinsing, patting, and drying, with the dish cloth now resembling a sanitary napkin, I wrestled the creature back into the plastic bag and into the washed vegetable bin of the refrigerator where it would *brine*.

I stirred the brine I'd made the day before, and poured it into the plastic bag. Quills had poked holes in the bag, so I muscled it back out again, and into the second bag I'd asked for at the *talho*. I poured the escaped pinkish brine in the crisper bin into the new bag, added another gallon of water so the body was more or less covered, managed to lift the bin, and to carry it back to the refrigerator, and only broke one small piece off the refrigerator´s bin collar while struggling to slide in the heavy bin. Turning, saw that I had created a hazmat zone. Everything the raw meat and its juice had touched had to be sanitized. I´d lent out my bucket of cleaning supplies, so all I had now as defense against botulism was blue Fairy dish soap, and white vinegar. I wiped everything down, removed my apron, shimmied sideways through the kitchen doorway and the refrigerator back out in search of forks, where I discovered northern Portugal's critical fork shortage. At six houseware stores I saw rows of gleaming knives and spoons. They could be bought individually or in sets, but there were no forks. At 11 o'clock at night I finally found forks in the houseware aisle in Porto's Froiz grocery store. The same mirror-finish as my *feira* wooden-handled cutlery, likewise made in Portugal, they sort-of matched.

The dinner turned out fine. Everyone fit around the extra tables that my friend, Jamie had helped me rent. The Christmas tree lights and red tealight candles made the atmosphere cozy. The turkey was moist. But I have to say I was very disappointed with the guests. Not one of the Danes, Swedes, Portuguese, or Goans had read the American National Turkey Federation's "Turkey 101." If they had, they had skimmed over the recommendation to eat one-and-one half pounds of turkey per person. As a plus, they were not sluggish from overeating though, so they bustled around cleaning my kitchen, and putting all the leftovers away so it was all clean in 15 minutes. I still have all this food in my freezer. I have half the turkey. One whole breast remained untouched by those 19 people.

I may not have known João well. I can´t say that anyone really did. I never knew if he preferred Naked Necks, Crested Breeds, Bantams, or his own species, or whether he was a leg man or a breast man. From his bruising though I can tell you that João was a spirited bird, full of life, and a fighter to the end. And next year when I lay him out again, I can say with complete authority that he was *aged on the premises*.

I Wonder As I Wander

Across the street from where I bunked is the Minho River, but actually it shows up everywhere like a kindly elder statesperson. The Minho River is very much like Marcelo Rebelo de Sousa, the president of the Portuguese Republic. The river wanders all over town, remaining visible from every vantage point.

And there are mountains here. Ahead of me off to the left are tall pine and beech trees. On the other side of the river is a mountain shrouded in mist. That is Spain. I am now walking in Portugal. This area is known as Western Galicia, and also the Iberian Peninsula. Galicia has a distinct and autonomous language and culture in northwestern Spain. The mountains are the Pyrenees, but also, the Calabrian Mountains bust through here and there. The two mountain chains are very similar, one being granite, gneiss, and limestone, and the other being granite and limestone. They constantly one-up each other, like the arguably similar Spanish and Portuguese people do. (This comment can be taken as a show of an outsider's ignorance, one who knows nothing.) The Galician name for the range of mountains which straddles the border between Spain and Portugal is *Serra do Xurés*. The Portuguese call it *Gerês*.

I made a brief trip north from the city of Porto to the town of Caminha. This is not the same as going *On the Caminho*, a religious pilgrimage which many people I know have done including my niece, Cecily, and which I have zero interest in doing. I'm usually happy just walking to the *frutaria*. But seven months into the international health crisis known as *the pandemic* I felt I needed a mental health break. These are times when everyone could use a vacation, but there is nowhere to go. Most sensible countries have closed their borders to try and control the spread as they sort things out. Other countries closed their public health ministries, and opened their borders to let in anyone with money to spend. Many people live in countries with priorities other than their citizens' welfare, and their citizens now have no money to eat or pay rent, let alone to travel, at least not by choice. (They may soon join throngs of homeless migrants, not a choice-type of travel.)

Being risk-averse I stayed in-country, only going north to the countryside away from the city, where there is a mountain and a river, and also, an ocean mouth, and where I was promised a good dinner and wine with friends. The dinner was quite delicious, at an Italian seafood place run by a husband and wife. My friends were lively and attentive. The place I am staying is a four-star hotel with a swimming pool. But I saunter just across the street and soon I am off the narrow, paved path that lurches above a sandy fringe bordering half a dozen or more small wooden fishing boats. I´m on a wooden boardwalk. The boardwalk has some boards recently replaced, and others bleached, and worn smooth. I take off my shoes. The river is wide like a lake.

Most of the fishing boats are painted red with black trim. In an act of rebellion some child has removed her socks and left the tiny pair blinking in the sunshine. Another child, a girl I gauge to be eight, rides by me furiously on the high wooden boardwalk with no railing bordering the rocky beach. She stomps her brakes suddenly fifteen meters ahead and looks over her shoulder for her father. Her father is walking quickly to keep up, but working very hard at appearing unconcerned. The girl's father passes me. We smile quickly as he moves on, concentrating on both his speed and his nonchalance. The girl has black hair cut in a bob with bangs. She looks very much like a painted "China Girl" on a decorative object, like maybe a child's pencil box.

Heart-achingly fragile wooden docks appear on my right, made of a mix of scrap lumber and scraped timber boughs. They remind me of birds' nests woven together of found fibers, and these docks are standing up from the river on two spindly long legs of tree boughs, mostly scraped bare, but some with patches of bark. I find these incredibly beautiful. Up ahead at the forest's edge I arrive at the taxi boat to go across the river to Spain. The boatman is standing next to an old wooden picnic table. In the center of the table is a very large gourd the color of muslin. I ask the boatman for a ride across the river, but he says that he cannot take me, he must call his *chefe*. He calls his chefe, and to make small talk as I wait I comment on the gourd. He pulls out his phone immediately and shows me pictures of his garden, leaning very close to me. He is smelling my perfume. Today I am wearing

Escada perfume, and a knee-length, wrap-around skirt with a ruffle, and I must look much better than usual. The boatman is about my age, and not bad looking for a boatman, nor for a man our age, and I find his flirting funny and flattering. I tell the boatman how much I like this area, how much I like his garden, and how much I needed to get out of Porto. He tells me that he much prefers Lisbon to Porto *for the light, and the life* and that Porto is *cinzento*, too grey. This boatman seems quite artistic.

The chefe arrives. I am surprised to see that he is a man at least fifteen years younger than the boatman. But, the chefe is a bitter man, and seems old already, or at least trying to get old. The chefe takes my proffered 10-euro note, and when I wait hand out for my five-euro change he says, "For the return trip." The two men help me into the swaying boat, and onto a red leatherette padded bar that goes across the boat. They tell me to sit astride it. If I'd worn any other kind of skirt that day than a wrap-around I would have had to hike it up, exposing my butt, which would have looked a lot like that gourd, only more symmetrical. The trip was short and miserable. The chefe hit all the wakes head-on so that it was impossible to sightsee. I'd had to grip the bench with all the strength in my thighs, and with both hands and my upper arms too, just not to get bucked off into the water. If my jaw had been allowed to open I would have bit my lip and possibly cracked teeth on the down strokes. I imagine it was similar to riding a bull. When I glanced back at the chefe he appeared to be acting the part of a boat captain ferrying spies in the dead of night. He frowned at the water as if on the lookout for enemy mines.

He motored into a remote-looking beach. He offered no assistance whatsoever to help me climb out, but sat glumly staring at the water. Holding my skirt, I crawled over the bow, and dropped down into calf-deep water. Asking for my five euros back seemed like asking for trouble, so I considered it a loss. I saw a reassuring wooden boardwalk and just barely visible ahead through the trees, a cantilevered white building with a turret. I carried my wet leather sandals. The sand felt good, and I hoped any splinters the beaten boardwalk might have had had been beaten down by the perpetual sea spray. They were even now damp in the sun. A woman about my age was wandering alone in the woods. She looked about hesitantly, or maybe wonderingly. We did not say anything to each other, maybe because we did not know what languages we each might speak, and maybe because the flutter of leaves, the slapping of waves, the sporadic bird twitter, and the crunching of sand beneath out feet was enough.

I followed the boardwalk through the forest and wound up at the hotel El Molino. I am in Spain now. It looks very new, and quirky. On the front of the turret is a windmill. The hotel has its own beach and a rustic snack bar, and outside a clean, modern bathroom, which I use. Behind the hotel is a small roundabout with a flagpole at the center. The new road leads to a sparse settlement of new-looking houses in various styles suggesting the lots were sold, and people built whatever they wanted on them. I go into the hotel and ask at the desk for a taxi—a land, not a water taxi - to get me to Laguardia. The town is several kilometers away so I cannot really walk. As I wait for the taxi I learn that the rooms here are only 50 euros per night compared to the 150 I have paid for my room at the spartan Porto do Sol on the Portuguese side of the river, where the only great thing is the bacon, which is seasoned with cloves. The orange juice tastes made from a mix, like Tang.

The taxi driver drops me where I ask to be dropped in Laguardia, on a small *praça*. People are out and about. Cheery pop music is playing from speakers on the praça. Children bicycle in the praça, which is paved with the same granite that the Portuguese pave every green surface with. There are nicely spaced magnolia trees offering shade, however all the stores are closed, except a few cafés. I guess people are doing just what I'm doing: getting out for air, exercise, and people-watching. I climb up the hill to a taxi stand and get in a taxi. After a taxi ride costing ten euros for a less than five kilometers, I leap out of the taxi as the man prepares to turn, and drive me several more blocks. (I found there were no ride-shares operating in Laguardia. The taxis have a monopoly.) I continued walking until I see a lively bar, marked "BAR." A tattooed young waitress with a partly shaved head and a rooster's cox comb in front showed me where to sit and plug in my phone, and gave me the wifi password: *Movistar*. She served me an Americano accompanied by a pitcher of molten-hot chocolate syrup. It was the best coffee I have ever had. Then I spied two pillowy croissants the size of a very large man's hand in a glass case at the bar in front of a very large man, the owner. I ordered one, and ate it, then went back for the second. I ripped them, and stuffed them into my mouth between sips of my chocolatey coffee, which I adjusted from time to time with more of the molten chocolate from the tiny white pitcher. My elbows rested on my knees as I leaned forward over the low coffee table in front of the banquette near the open door. The waitress called me a taxi, and a smiling man appeared who wanted twenty euros to take me back to the other side of the river, a trip that in Porto would be less than half that price, even in an official taxi. I offered him twelve. He said he could *not afford it*. He and the owner and the waitress had a big conversation over the coffee he could afford, and I heard the waitress defending me with, "She's American. She's nice," but the taxi driver finally got up off his bar stool, gave me a goodbye and a friendly thumbs-up, and got into his car and drove away.

I walked to another bar around the corner and waited while the waiter carried trays of coffee and more giant, fluffy, butter croissants. These Spanish know how to make croissants, and coffee with chocolate! The waiter called a taxi that also wanted twenty euros. So, I began walking toward Portugal. My phone navigation indicated that it was a three-and-a-half-hour walk. The day was warm and pleasant. I had on the comfortable sandals, now more or less dry, that Teri, my Foz friend, took me to buy at Seaside. I had no intention of walking three and a half hours, and would also miss my train in that time.

I left the town area and entered a highway overpass into a sparsely-populated residential area following my phone navigation. I prepared myself mentally to walk up one of the long, hillside driveways to a stranger's door, knock, and ask any way I could if they knew anyone who would take me back to Portugal, hoping for the best. I am getting a bit desperate as I have a return train to catch from the other side of the river, and I must get back to the hotel and retrieve my suitcase first. Instead, I came upon a fire station up a very short hill, almost level with the road. I walked in through the gate to a parking lot and as I approached the glass door a tall and gorgeous man with a shaved head came out. I explained in Portuguese and in English that I had no car, and asked if he could call someone to take me over the river to Portugal. It took a bit of explaining because the fireman did not speak either of those languages. There are three distinct dialects in Galicia, which developed differently due to the isolating geography of the mountains, just as in Appalachia there are distinct cultural pockets, or "hollers" between mountains. One young Tennessee boy I met on a train told my husband and daughter and I he lived in "the holler" when we asked where he was from. The fireman probably spoke all three dialects, given his job. He said, *One moment*, or something like that, went back inside, came out instantly with keys, locked the fire station door, and said *Hop in,* or something like that.

As it was now apparent that he was the only fireman working at that time, I was horrified. *What if there is a fire?* I exclaimed. My arms rose, demonstrating monstrous flames. I used the word *incendeirio*. I wanted a ride to Portugal, but not at the expense of burning down a village.

Aw! Come on! he said. That's the Australian version, not exactly as he said it, but close enough. We hopped into his large white SUV. He drove around curves like a corkscrew down to the bottom of the hill to a ferry boat station and he told me to wait. I climbed down after him, and followed him inside where I heard him tell the dispatch woman that I needed passage. She said *1.50* and she told me to go with the fireman *mais rápido!* We climbed back up into his truck. The fireman drove now like mad back up to the street, and down a long roadway, up to the ferry gate at the boat itself, which was already loaded. Three wiry, tan, and leathery men were waiting for me before they closed the big metal gate, which was steel like an oversized truck tailgate, and once painted a bright, grass green. The Galician fireman replied *De nada,* to my Portuguese and American thank-yous. Over his pandemic face mask his eyes looked just like warm, melted chocolate.

One of the lean ferrymen in a lime-green sport shirt tore my paper ticket, which was like a tiny, thin grocery store receipt. He handed me back half, less than an inch long. The men closed the gate, and I wove through the cars, and up a red painted metal staircase, selecting a seat on the double row of white plastic bucket seats that were half-filled with families. In five minutes we arrived on the other side, with no wakes and no theatrics. A little ways ahead, across the street I spied the fishing supplies store I'd first stopped at after dragging my suitcase up the hill from the train station. It looked familiar. With its fishing rods leaning against the outside wall, its hanging, patterned sweaters, wading boots, and nets it reminded me of Haddrell's Point in The Old Village of Mount Pleasant, South Carolina. I'd spoken to the family that ran this store as I waited for the taxi the hotel had sent for me. This time I called the hotel taxi driver, Sérgio, directly. Sérgio came quickly to the ferry. We drove along the winding mountain highway from Caminha to Vila Nova de Cerveira, where there was time for him to drop me at a large, open *praça* where diners were seated at small tables under umbrellas to shield them from the sun while enjoying an infectious drum beat.

The drum group is three women and two men, their backs to the wall of a building. They sway athletically back and forth swinging mallets in sync, the three women bookended by the two men, and all wear the same black T-shirts with a neon green logo, and demure, knee-length black shorts. The drums are all neon green. Walking normally across the *praça* seemed absurd, so I stopped fighting my urge to dance and began to bop along with the music, and when I put my only coin into the upturned conga drum in front of the group, a smile lit up the faces of all five players synchronously, too. I bopped on toward the *feira* to pick up a souvenir of my mini sojourn, passing a larger than life–sized crocheted peacock in purples, set in a mowed field, a life-sized piano crocheted in vivid colors, its crocheted performer attired in a Prince-like outfit, and a giant crocheted guitar. All seemed brighter than life in the white August sunshine.

The *feira* I approached from above, looking down on a sea of white tents. I found steps down a little way past, and passed three pleasant police officers, one struggling to screw the top on a liter plastic spray bottle of hand sanitizer. All the shoppers waited for the officer to get the sanitizer ready, and then passed in an orderly fashion through this entrance, waiting for their hands to be squirted. Down the short flight of steps separated down the middle by a rope, one side for *Entrada,* the other for *Saída,* we entered the *feira*. This *feira* is much more organized than the *feiras* I know in Porto, the town for example providing the vendors with uniform white tents. It has much wider aisles, and much wider stalls. Some of the stalls are really complete, organized, huge shops. One shop I stopped at had every type of basket imaginable, and also woven natural willow or reed or grass lampshades, arm chairs, and covered hampers, as well as the Moroccan shopping baskets with leather handles I love, but here they had some so large they would be impossible to lift when filled. Were they for storage of kindling? They had all sizes of the lustrous, honey-brown willow, double-hinge-lidded Portuguese picnic baskets lined in red and white or blue and white gingham-checked cotton. Hanging from long straps of leather on slats underneath the uniform white awnings were fanciful bags of fine woven grass dyed in indigo, magenta, lime, and yellow from Madagascar.

In a kitchen store that would shame the US chains, Crate and Barrel, and Williams Sonoma, (where I´ve bought Portuguese ceramics over the years) I bought two heavy ten-inch chef's knives, Nicil brand, after searching for a carbon steel knife so I could retire my forty-year-old Sabatier. The knives were marked twenty-two euros each, but without my asking the proprietor reduced my price to twenty, moved by the story of how my mother had bought the Sabatier to help me open a café, and how I've used this knife every day since, carting it with me wherever I have stayed for more than a few weeks. I also bought from her two beautifully boxed, elegant, elongated ovals of locally mined whetstone for 1.50 each. The only other thing I buy is a papier–mâché toy, an angel with stiff, yellow wings protruding from a pale blue hospital gown, with fists raised, a COVID hero I find funny and brave and endearing.

I call Sérgio the taxi driver when I am ready to leave and he arrives minutes later in this small town. He takes me to the Porto do Sol where I pick up my suitcase in the lobby as he waits to take me to the train station. I leave Caminha by train, as I arrived. Because I am recognized as a senior citizen now, I receive the discounted train ticket price of only 4.95 for the pleasant two-hour ride. The small white train station is decorated with hand-painted blue and white tiles depicting rustic work scenes, and these tiles are bordered in feminine, hand-painted tiles of yellow and green garlands of flowers and leaves. There is a group of us, and as the time for the Porto train to arrive approaches, we troop across to the other side of the tracks; teens, and a woman with a wheelbarrow, who continues along the quay. A woman with waist-length, coppery-gold hair in a long, crisp salmon-colored dress scoots aside to share her bench with me. With her wavy long hair and long dress, she looks like a magical storybook princess. Really, she is a normal Brazilian woman. We sit in the late afternoon sun a *social distance* apart, admiring the tiles together from across the tracks. I point to the station gable's lace gingerbread, how it looks like daisy flowers, (called *margaridas*) and she says that all the stations along the Douro line are *beautiful*. I tell her I admire her dress very much, and she tells me where she bought it, at a store called Umi, on sale, and because we were both there early, I open my suitcase to show her my new dress of white linen, which no matter how deeply I rummage I cannot find. In a panic I realize I'd left it behind in the hotel, where it was invisible against the crumpled white sheets, when I packed quickly. She helped me put everything back into my suitcase, and press down the top to help me zip it. After I called the hotel and asked the desk clerk to look for my dress in the room, I help the woman order my white linen dress for herself using my phone, after comparing our body sizes and deciding what is her correct size. (The dress is from La Redoute and I have since ordered many things from here, while shops are closed. I love their customer service as returns are free and refunds arrive in a day or two.)

The train arrives. We separate, she going left and me going right, and too upset about my dress to converse more. (One week later the hotel sends me my dress!) The trains are being run at reduced capacity by one-third to reduce COVID infection. The seats are comfortable. Everyone wears a mask. Two-thirds of the passengers are mothers with children dozing, fathers holding children on their laps. I am surrounded by families calmed by a day in the sun, surrounded by green mountains, and white buildings and blue river and winking sea. This is a quality of life that everyday people can afford to give their children in Portugal. How I wish American families could someday know this peace again. Most of the families get off at Viana do Castelo. Another family gets on with an enormous blue and white carousel horse. It is really nothing but a plastic balloon. But the little girl adores it. I wonder how long it will be before it slowly loses its air and becomes a wrinkled bit of foul-smelling refuse.

One would hope this international health crisis was uniting the world in solidarity. On the upside, I can see how children love having their parents at home, and how parents who can survive financially must love sleeping late, and remembering who they are and who they belong to. Not a boss, not a company, not a corporation, not a government. This could actually be some sort of turning point.

António's Stick

António's stick is long. Its girth is consistent from one end to the other, except at the tip, where it is slightly pointed like a fence post. It is firm and hard.

António is a short man. Because of his love of simple carbohydrates, António is soft around the middle. (I must admit that I also eat his cookies.)

Each Sunday a bevy of beauties congregates at António's house. We ring the buzzer at the appointed time. António comes to open the gate. He wears a plaid shirt, loose, worn denim jeans,

ANTÓNIO'S STICK

and a deerskin jacket worn thin, without fringe. We arrive wearing sundresses. Or, diaphanous swim-suit coverups. Nothing is fashionable about António. This is something I find irresistible.

António's house, his gardens, his swimming pool, and his pool pavilion are one block from the ocean in the city's most fashionable village. The weather remains deliciously cool here even in August heat. We swim a few strokes. We dip. We lay down in his lounge chairs. We splay on his carpet of spongey, green grass on towels we lay down. Under, his grass is some special kind. It is like a thick, heavily napped woven Persian carpet in only one color: green.

António turns on his in-ground sprinkler system first thing in the morning on waking, before he makes coffee. He watches the birds drink and play in the water. Little *andorinhas,* and sometimes, *hoopoes.* Wild rabbits and a feral chicken show up from the woods now and then.

António makes coffee in a battered Turkish pot. We all hate his coffee, yet we don't complain.

The Triplets are welcome to come here. The Triplets are three young, annoying dogs, siblings that have been farmed out to homes in the neighborhood, foundlings - that pointed, petite-style dog that does nothing for me. The dogs play-fight each other vying for our attention. They dig in António's begonia beds. António's actual bed is so large that it can sleep four. Humans. The dogs stay outside, and watch us through the windows.

Flora is António's dog. She is *nothing* like the others. Flora is a boxer. Flora is the Lauren Hutton of boxers, an ageless, effortless beauty, who has seen it all. She barely bothers to roll her eyes. Flora is the best boxer in the world. I tell her this, feeling with two hands her muscle layer spread over the broad rib cage. Her shiny, burnt-caramel-colored coat is like a different vein of gold. Flora is fourteen. We drink to each other

ANTÓNIO'S STICK

only with thine eyes for a long, long time, feeling no shame or embarrassment whatsoever. Flora's eyes are brown, and moist, and protruding. Like any boxer, I guess.

At least half of the bevy of beauties ogle António's stick. We all carry serious books, but no one is really here to read. I also bring *Mad* magazine, and *Rolling Stone* magazine, because I cannot concentrate, and I am really bad at pretending. I think of what will happen behind the back wall, in the wild area in front of the woods. I think of the sound of the wind in the trees that blocks out all other sounds. No one speaks much in front of the woods. By the pool in front, neglected authors lie crisping in the sun, their spines splayed.

António has exited the house. He carries a small yellow glass pitcher the color and opacity of Vaseline. It holds plain tap water. In his other hand he holds tiny glasses, childrens' juice glasses.

We are lolling on the carpet, some of us barely covered in tiny, tiny bikinis. António still wears his deerskin jacket. Only once have I seen António outside wearing swimming trunks. His skin is pale white speckled with gold. António has dry skin. Because of this he does not go in his pool.

We all get up from lolling as if on cue. We go through the motions of pouring water into the tiny glasses, and sip.

When António is excited, his eyes become large. His voice rises, *Come! Come!* he says in English, for my benefit. We've now finished our water. António walks us behind the first wall, which is tiled yellow, grey, and white and looks vaguely Mondrian, but sedate. He leads us past the sauna, past the dusty rubber trees struggling for light in pumice stone planters, and through the glass door into another small garden. Here there is a high, ceramic round table with the names of his children and late wife baked into the clay as place settings. We walk past it and to another wall. This wall is ancient stone. António has cleverly cut a rectangular opening into the wall, which he covered with a door on a sliding track, a door of insulation board in between aluminum skins, which he covers behind us, and we are in a wild, hidden world cut off from any other. Only the sound of the wind in the trees—*susurrous, psithuros*—can be heard.

We beauties trail António like fallen cherry blossoms from a wind-shaken tree. António's shed looks on impassively. We stand next to furrows in a casual nursery with pale green baby gingko bilobas lying in the furrows to wet them and taller, shiny red blueberry bushes, thigh-high, to shelter them. There is one big, tall black and craggy tree. One bikini-clad beauty whose name is Aurora tells me that this is a black willow tree. It looks nothing like a weeping willow. Its leaves are spitefully small—erect like cropped ears of a dog made to look cruel. Perhaps this tree pities no one.

We float on a wafting lower breeze around António, circling closely. António takes out his stick. He swings it around like a Samurai sword and we move as required. He tells us his stick is his *COVID-19 social distance meter*. This is a great joke, as the government regulations are social distance must be two meters. We murmur sonorously, our voices blending and dispersing in the wind then coming back to us like foreign bird twitter.

Finished, I go on further beyond the nursery. I don't care where the others go. Beyond the nursery is the woods. The second time I went back there in my bathing suit I got lost, climbing over branches tangled into barricades. Then, I saw the blackberries peeping and twinkling at me, shoulder height and down to my knees. I picked them. All the feral chickens and rabbits were napping. I took what I wanted. Reluctantly I found my way back, jangling a few berries in my hat to make my absence justified. We took turns tossing berries to the dogs.

ANTÓNIO'S STICK

The next time I come António hands me a scarred glass bowl the size of a melon cut in half. I prefer my hat, and I prefer to go to the woods alone with no one expecting anything from me.

After, we always go inside the house and eat. The house is dark and filled with art. We order pizza most days, and eat salad António's *empregada* makes him in advance. She does not come here Sundays. António's empregada is madly in love with him. I can tell this from the salads she makes him. She suffers, working a treacherous mandolina, slicing raw beets transparent as inner flesh. She minces the carrots into colorful ticks of confetti. As António slices her tomatoes for us with a sharp knife. He tells us that she has grown these tomatoes in her own garden.

One Sunday he serves us soup. He has made the soup from a chicken his empregada raised and killed just for him. The soup is just chicken, water, and salt. My bowl is shallow with the broth and a whole leg sticking out of the broth. I'm not sure where to put this bone.

Each week António makes sangria. Each week the sangria becomes more delicious.

Forgive me if you think this is something I should have mentioned earlier—António is a wood merchant. His stick lay buried for five thousand years in the Netherlands at the bottom of a canal. It is quite unique. The stick is a very dark wood.

In seventy-five years in the wood import and milling business António has never lost his love of wood; wood living and wood dead. This honest sense of wonder I love about António.

António's bed is in a downstairs suite. We change our swimming costumes in there. His neighbor I met at yoga. She organized the bevy.

ANTÓNIO'S STICK

There is a secret ingredient in António's sangria, which I can't tell you. Okay, I will tell you: *banana*.

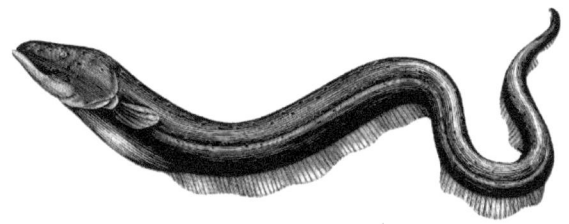

The Portuguese Model of Physiotherapy

ABSTRACT

This study looks at the Portuguese model of physiotherapy and attempts to answer the question: How well does the Portuguese model of physiotherapy address the goals of physiotherapy?

INTRODUCTION

Goals of physiotherapy have been identified by The National Institutes of Health (United States) as "a reduction in pain, increased range of motion, increased endurance and strength, restored independence, a reduction in stress, and a greater quality of life for the patients." To this already seemingly ambitious set of objectives the Associação Portuguesa de Fisioterapeutas adds goals of "psychological, emotional, and social well-being."

Hippocrates of Kos, Greece in 460 BC, and Persian, Chinese, and Egyptian medical practitioners at about the same time are recorded prescribing exercise, movement, dance, and therapeutic massage for pain relief. Hydrotherapy, physiotherapy using water, was also recorded at this time in Greece. The Romans discovered Portugal's naturally-occurring therapeutic thermal springs, and made extensive use of their healing powers. Some of these ancient springs are in use today. During the 19th century some were transformed into modern spas offering additional physiotherapies, and other services, such as nutrition counselling. In 1921, Mary McMillan established the American Women's Physical Therapeutic Association. This later became the American Physical Therapy Association. Portugal's Associação Portuguesa de

Fisioterapeutas (APFISIO) was established in 1953.

Until the 1960s there were only a few dozen licensed physiotherapists practicing in Portugal, and today there are over 12,000. The country's labor-intensive industries, including farming, fishing, manufacturing, and sports, and the popularity of hard-paving surfaces in concrete, stone and tile, including institutions, private homes, and children's playparks provide an endless supply of physiotherapy patients.

Most physiologists in Portugal work in private practice outside of hospitals. Their clinics may be distinguished by colorful window wraps or posters depicting people of various demographics sitting or lying on a table. Michelangelo's Vitruvian Man also makes the odd appearance. The wraps are used by other businesses, including dentistry, insurance, engineering, gymnastics and massage studios, but given the relatively high ratio of 1:833

physiotherapists to residents, one may safely assume physiotherapy services are offered behind such posters unless one is greeted by a topless, corseted woman holding a riding crop, (as actually occurred to the Researcher at the onset of this study.)

The APFISIO website features a Forbes study ranking physiotherapy #3 of all professional occupations in terms of offering its practitioners "the most happiness."

METHODOLOGY

The "Advocacy/Participatory Worldview" allows researchers to "engage the participants as active collaborators in their inquiries." (Creswell 2009.) The "socially constructed nature of reality, the intimate relationship between the researcher and what is studied," and the "situational constraints that shape inquiry" are characteristic of qualitative research. (Denzin & Lincoln 2005).

The intimate relationship between Denzin & Lincoln (if any) is not known. The Researcher and the Primary Subject in this study were physically intimate on a daily basis. The Researcher´s Primary Subjects are herself, and her Right Hand. Pains were taken to maintain objectivity. To differentiate the role of the Researcher from her Primary Subjects, the latter two are identified as "PS," and "H".

King (2011) advises research "methods and substance must be connected." The Researcher/PS broke her Right Hand (H). Of critical interest were methods of:

- holding a pen

- typing

- holding a spoon level long enough to place food in the mouth, and

- connecting substance of bone and muscle.

Situational constraints that shaped this inquiry include:

- Data collection was limited to a period of approximately* three months.

- Data collection was limited to Portugal.

- Data collection was limited to one physiotherapy clinic.

- Data collection was limited to one bone.

While a "lack of intellectual rigor" may be inferred from an unwellness on the part of the Researcher to break additional bones in additional countries for the study, the Researcher is not the one being judged here.

First-person exposition has been used to further understanding, although expletives have been redacted.

WEIRD FOODS OF PORTUGAL

THE SUBJECT AND THE STUDY GROUP

The Primary Subjects have been introduced as the Researcher (PS) and her Right Hand (H). The Secondary Study Group is comprised of other patients and staff at the physiotherapy clinic studied. Given the sensitive nature of the Results of this study, the name of the clinic, and its staff have been changed. The clinic will be called "S&M Fisio."

The Researcher is a mature American female (MAF). H is slender, prone to dryness, and freckled with age spots. On August 13, H was crushed between a concrete wall and a second MAF at a book club meeting. The second MAF tripped and fell onto the PS. H was holding a platter of Italian-American submarine sandwiches at the time. The PS shifted the platter to her other hand, employing H to catch the falling MAF. At the moment of impact, the PS reports hearing a loud crunch of bones, and screaming. (The PS reports that the sandwiches

THE PORTUGUESE MODEL OF PHYSIOTHERAPY

and the second MAF were unharmed. She asks that her "heroic actions" to save both be noted here.) The PS reports that a mature British female (MBF) standing equidistant, "holding nothing in her hands," did not move to assist, but said, "One should never try to catch someone when they fall. One will always get injured."

The PS reports hiding H under a tablecloth throughout a lengthy discussion of travel books, of which she recalls, "her book, Bruce Chatwin´s "In Patagonia", AND a religious tome presented by the group leader, a mature Canadian male, (MCM), because the subject of that book was "being transported to a higher plane of consciousness where pain is not felt." (The PS has requested "it be noted that she has Medis …insurance.)

Three days after the incident the PS was confronted by a domestic worker who asked, "Why is your hand hanging limp, like a sleeping bat?" PS was then admitted to *Urgências do Hospital Lusíadas*. The consulting orthopedic physician examined x-rays of H, concluding H's First Carpel Trapezoid was,"*Partido.*" (Portuguese medical jargon.) The physician splinted H onto the PS´ Second Carpel, bending both carpels at a forty-five-degree angle before casting them in a hard plaster substance. Five weekly visits to *Urgências do Hospital Lusíadas* followed. Care was provided by orthopedic physician Dr. André Rodrigues Pine Tree (his real name,) until Dr. Pine Tree determined that the bone had become reconnected. The PS reports,

> "This is a miracle because the radiologists—all big, meaty men, threw (H) violently onto the table each week, twisting my arm into an unnatural position as they forced me to kneel submissively in empty air....When the bandages came off for the final time I had not one defective finger, but two! It was as if both fingers were suffering from advanced osteoporosis, or a

night of heavy drinking. Neither was able to stand up straight.... Without support from the hard plaster, my hand hurt (redacted....) It was hideously swollen and discolored. I had to carry it in front of me wherever I went like a pitiful dead pet."

The PS reportedly called many physiology clinics, and reported that she physically entered into several places that appeared to be physiology clinics from the outside, which she found "misleadingly advertised." The only proper physiology clinic with availability that accepted insurance was S&M Fisio, which she found on the 4th of November. S&M Fisio agreed to see her immediately, and accepted her insurance, (*Medis.*)

Treatments occurred five days each week, with exceptions as noted in Arguments. The PS claims to be unaware of the exact date treatments were "unilaterally and abruptly ended," claiming to have blanked out the date under "trauma," but she believes it was sometime in January or February.

RESULTS

This study looks at the Portuguese model of physiotherapy and attempts to answer the question: How well does the Portuguese model of physiotherapy (PMP) address the goals of physiotherapy, which include "a reduction in pain, increased range of motion, increased endurance and strength, restored independence, a reduction in stress, a greater quality of life for the patients, and psychological, emotional, and social well-being."

Figure 1 shows at the end of treatments, the PS reported a "reduction in pain, increased range of motion, increased endurance and strength," (ROMES) and restored *physical* independence (INDE). The PS also complained of weight gain, correlated with a renewed dexterity with cooking and eating utensils. (No control study was conducted, and this is unverified.)

THE PORTUGUESE MODEL OF PHYSIOTHERAPY

An unexpected side effect of *psychological dependence* may have resulted from the treatments. A reduction in stress (STRESS) can be said to have been met with only partial success. Generalized anxiety, and "panic" over how she would fill her mornings once the daily therapy sessions ended were reported by the PS.

A greater quality of life (GQ) cannot definitively be shown to have been achieved by the Portuguese Model of Physiotherapy. APFISIO's psycho-social goals of psychological, emotional, and social well-being, (PESW) were met only temporarily, in so much as they were met at all.

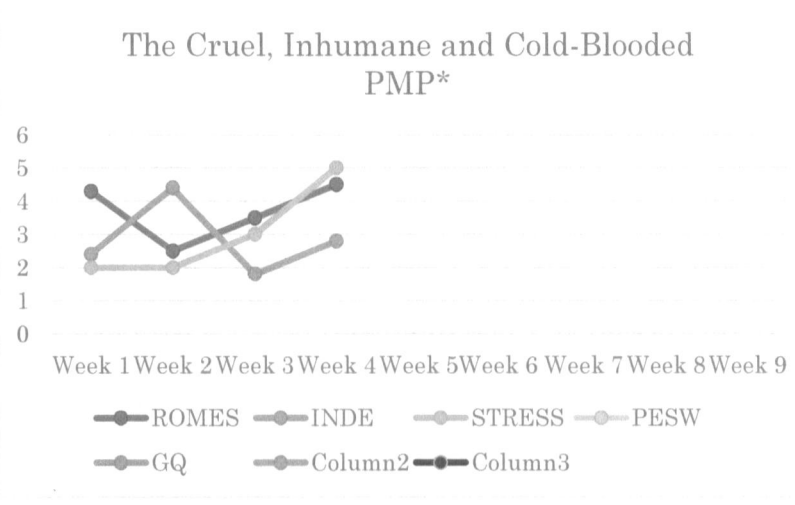

(Figure 1. *Chart labelling was done by the PS as a condition for her participation. There is no way the Researcher would have ever labelled a scientific chart in such an unprofessional way.)

ARGUMENTS

Consistent with a Qualitative methodology, and an Advocacy/Participatory Worldview, Arguments are presented in the Subject's voice.

WEEK 1: On my first visit to S&M Fisio I was struck by its shabbiness. On my third visit I intended never to return. Finding the place was a challenge. The address was a plain beige building maybe from the late 1950s, with an open airplane hangar in the center, without signage, or any address number. On the left side was a butcher shop. There always is. Cradling (H) I entered the hangar, passing a glassed-in area with mailboxes before seeing a small metal sign with the street number. Next to the sign was a deckle-edged piece of cardboard with a hand-drawn hieroglyphic of a staircase. The staircase had an arrow-point at the end, so I guessed it was a map to the street number. I followed left, back, left, back, and so on, passing a dress shop (with nothing I would ever wear in its windows,) continuing on to a glassed-in area with a circular metal staircase, and two elevators. There I eventually detected a brass-plated plaque the size of an A4 envelope at knee height with faint, cursive engraving: "Clínica."

The door to the stairwell was open. It was by now quite dark at this point so far from the street, and with no windows, and no artificial lighting on an overcast, and raining day. To celebrate my two functioning legs, I opted to take the circular staircase. I progressed in a tight corkscrew. It became much darker. At every other turn I could tell that I was on a short, shallow hallway. I detected doors on each end, but saw no lights, no signs and the doors were always locked.

By now it was possible to continue up the staircase only by dragging myself up along the metal handrail using my left hand. This left (H) unsupported and throbbing pitifully. In near-total blackness I looked down at gold specks in the white linoleum stair treads that occasionally twinkled when they caught and mirrored my purse buckle. This was necessary just to avoid becoming dizzy and collapsing. Finally, I saw a light up ahead, and an open doorway. I fell into the space gasping, into a small waiting area. Half a dozen people sat wedged elbow to elbow on metal chairs, all wearing overcoats. They looked up with mild curiosity. The air smelled of fresh laundry.

A woman with bright blond hair and half-glasses - who looked almost exactly like the actress, Patrícia Arquette – was behind a counter a few steps away, arguing on the telephone. When she saw me, she slammed down the phone, demanded my *Medis* insurance card, and €13.75, and told me to return the following morning at

THE PORTUGUESE MODEL OF PHYSIOTHERAPY

11. I fell back out into the stairwell past the bundle of people, and took the elevator down.

By following the light I was able to navigate my way out to the street and into the half-light of day. I saw a bus stop across the street. I saved close to €5 by taking the bus home.

The next morning I rode the Uber in, and rode the elevator up. As soon as I entered, I was told to follow a petite blonde in blue hospital scrubs. She led me down a narrow hallway lined in blue plastic shower curtains. People were moaning behind the curtains. We entered a room that can only be described as a mental asylum. A woman with an energetically swinging black ponytail was wiping the same square foot of wall again and again with a frayed towel. An elderly woman sat in a corner alone stacking children's blocks. A very frail, elderly woman in men´s socks and loose plaid trousers, wearing acetate wraparound sunglasses like a shield worn by welders was walking back and forth across a toddler´s brown vinyl mattress on the floor, running her hands along ancient galvanized pipe handrails at each side. People lay listless on brown vinyl cots along the wall. There were at least a dozen people in this small room which was lit only by the dim daylight from a window at one the end. The window looked out onto roof pipe vents.

I was directed to sit at a small table with a woman engrossed in laboriously sorting varnished wooden dowels, putting them into holes on a battered wooden board. She did not look up, and she moved as if heavily sedated. The table was at most 3 feet X 2 feet. Inches from the back of my chair were a wooden coat rack and a rolling metal cart.

The therapist in scrubs began nicely enough. Shyly she explained that she spoke no English. She had a twitching, half-smile. Her hands were very soft and smooth. She took up (H) gently, took a dab of Nivea cream from a small tin on the table, and tentatively moved the dab over

THE PORTUGUESE MODEL OF PHYSIOTHERAPY

(H). I winced in pain. The dowel-sorter looked up nervously. Each time I cried out, the therapist seemed to gain satisfaction; her smile widened and evened out. The other patients all kept their eyes averted.

A loud woman with wiry grey hair wearing hiking boots and a white medical coat entered. She began twisting the painfully thin arm of the elderly woman in men´s socks. I count fifteen people, and gauged this room to be at most fourteen feet by twenty-four feet.

On day three I arrived to firefighters, and a large crowd assembled in front of the building. Brushing past, I followed the hand-drawn hieroglyphic into the maze. At the second glassed-in stairwell the elevators were crossed-off with yellow hazard tape. Water poured down the spiral staircase. This was inside a building. A man in a dress hat, with an opened umbrella came walking calmly down the steps, water pouring on his umbrella and rushing under his feet. This was like the Max Ernst absurdist painting come to life. (Researcher note: The PS is probably referencing artist Rene Magritte, not Ernst. Magritte and Ernst were *surrealists*, not *absurdists*.)

Assuming the roof had collapsed under the long period of heavy rains I left quickly, fearing that if I stayed much longer I would be either electrocuted or crushed.

[H] was so weak I was unable to hold a pen or type, except with my left hand. This changed my two-fingered peck into a one-fingered peck with at least one typo per word. I tried using the computer's voice transcription program, but a cartoon character shaped like a paper clip popped up accusingly, announcing "Sleeping" whenever I stopped speaking for a second to think. This constant disapproval, telling me in effect that I was mentally sluggish, on top of being physically impaired was more than I could bear. I waited seven days. No one from the clinic called or emailed me to ask where I was or to

THE PORTUGUESE MODEL OF PHYSIOTHERAPY

explain the building collapse. I assumed they were all dead. With dread and no other choice, I reluctantly returned to the clinic.

The blond at the desk, *Cruella, shrugged when I asked what had happened. She said the water heater had broken, and that S&M Fisio had remained open the whole time.

WEEK 2: The petite blonde therapist is *Aella Mara. The grey-haired woman in hiking boots is *Nurse Ratched. I sit in the same slot every day between the coat rack and metal rolling cart across from the dowel-sorter. It is always 11 a.m. The tools are always arranged on a thick, grey plastic sheet on the small table with the Nivea tin, and a stack of crispy, paper cocktail napkins. My tools are a tub of spearmint-colored Silly Putty marked "Rep Putty," rubber bands commonly used around broccoli, a sand-colored infant's toy football in foam with a few flecks of its blue rubber coating remaining, and a hard blue foam piece the size of a stogie cigar. I do 10 minutes of football squeezing, 10 minutes of rubber band stretching, and 10 minutes of stogie squeezing. Then Aella Mara comes to manipulate (H). (H) is swollen from edema. Every touch is painful.

At a certain point, a man comes out from behind a curtain at the far end of the room and sits down next to me. He must sit sideways facing out to avoid touching me or knocking his knees into the dowel-sorter's knees. His arm is always wrapped in a white towel. No one ever says anything to him, and he never says anything, either. No one here says much of anything to anyone. He looks around the room very observantly, with large, intelligent eyes. He is trim, with a compact body and long limbs. He seems quite sentient.

By now the other patients scoot aside each morning in the small waiting area to let me squeeze in with them. A heat-induced narcolepsy pervades the air. Is it from a multi-storied commercial laundry facility behind all those locked doors? The smell of the fresh laundry is intoxicating.

I do not want to imagine what is going on behind those blue curtains I pass every day as every possible indignity is happening right in plain sight in the common room. Walls are covered in nunchucks, horse-riding stirrups, and a welded metal wheel with a protruding handle. (I looked up "Medieval torture wheel" and immediately regretted it.) Aella Mara resembles the Wheel of Fortune game show host, Vanna White, if White had an evil twin.

Aella Mara has bottomless, frightening, black eyes. I realize that her hair is dyed blond. Is she a Gypsy? It is best that I not speak to her because my torturous Portuguese only seems to agitate her. Then she presses more ruthlessly on my fragile bones and purple edema.

Today when I cried out in pain my elderly dowel-sorting neighbor looked up. She called my therapist, "Santa *Aella." I recognized this right away as irony. I think she spoke for the first time to notify Aella Mara that she is being watched, so that she does not seriously hurt either one of us. The woman with the swinging black ponytail who wipes the wall is not insane, but Brazilian. I deduce this from her tropical outfits of shrunken tank tops, tight pastel jeans, and sandals, and the fact that no one speaks to her either. Her body is so curvy it would accurately be described as bulbous. Her injury is work-related? A bar fight?

WEEK 3: Nurse Ratched continues to tyrannize the other patients, but she leaves me alone. I sense that because I am new here, and American the atmosphere is more subdued than normal. This only piques my journalistic curiosity. (Researcher note: A journalism degree from Stephens College was conferred on the PS in 1986.) The man who joins us at our table with the towel around his arm wears a green sweater every day. I realize that who he reminds me of is Kermit the Frog. Our dowel-sorting table-mate is Laurinda. Each day at the same time the man appears from the back of the room, his arm wrapped in the towel. He sits sideways with us for ten, or maybe it is twenty minutes, observes the room silently, then slips away.

There is an unspoken patient dress code of pullover sweaters, and dress slacks in subdued colors; navy blue, brown, maroon, or grey with only slight variations; a discreet argyle here, a stripe there, "Kermit´s" brighter green sweater. Men and women alike dress this way. The mattress walker is Margarida. I´ve never seen her without her dark eye shield, despite the only light in the room coming from the one window. Margarida is the coolest one here. She gets me. She has started a group-speak based on gestures, as if I am deaf, and not simply American. We all now mimic her characteristic shoulder shrugs, and Chaplin-esque upturned palms. The rare times that any of us speak, (she never speaks,) we speak in single words. Never more than three together. We focus on nouns, although the adjective, *melhor* (better) we share for group morale building. Beyond the roof vent pipes I notice a line of golden yellow tree tops in the distance.

After a week everyone knows their routine. After two weeks everyone knows each other's. Sandra, the heavy-set woman also always wears sunglasses, which I now recognize as a form of politeness since we are all so smashed together, seems to have more money than the rest of us. At least she has a larger wardrobe. Each day she wears a different muted pullover sweater and slacks. I picture her dressing carefully for our benefit each morning. She seems to know English, as she is always looking my way smiling, waiting for my reactions to the small things going on. She lies on one of the brown cots along the wall waiting for an electrical device to be strapped to her foot. After that, she comes to the stool behind Laurinda, and waits for Rachel,

THE PORTUGUESE MODEL OF PHYSIOTHERAPY

(her real name) the sweet, young, dark-haired therapist to bring her tub of warm water that she soaks her foot in.

Rachel always brings her equipment. I am always served by Aella Mara. The radio is always tuned to a mixture of American pop tune covers that sound similar to the originals from the 1980s, and more recent Brazilian and Portuguese pop. The volume is always set at the exact volume that can be either ignored or enjoyed, depending on one´s mood and preferences. Sometimes Aella Mara sings along. She wears small faceted teardrop earrings that glitter and bob while she manipulates my hand. A new guy arrived today. Tall and distinguished with hooded Patrícian eyes, and lustrous, wavy silver hair. He wore a white-collared dress shirt, and an expensive-looking dark, tailored suit jacket. We all sat up straighter. We think he is very elegant, and elevates our group. His name is Arturo.

WEEK 4: A new woman arrived, heavily made up in face powder, a *coiffure*, and wearing a real fur coat, if you can believe that. She seemed overly interested in Arturo. We didn't like her. I´m not sure who did what to her, but we got rid of her in two days.

Patrícia is a younger patient. Like the Brazilian, she is allowed to deviate from our dress code. She wears tight jeans, knee-high boots, and a light-colored coat trimmed in fake fur. (The Brazilian wears no coat.) Patrícia brings her three children each day. They sit in the waiting area with Sandra´s husband. Her daughter is eleven; oblivious to the surroundings, reading on her phone. Her brother is nine, also serious, but alert to the surroundings, because it is his job to mind their little brother, who is four, and a terror.

Sandra's husband seems to really enjoy this job. Cruella has an assistant, José (his real name.) José manages patient records on old-fashioned index cards. He is very tall, young, and bashfully sweet-faced. He carries his stack of cards up from some office down the back hall, and towers over Cruella´s counter hunching over the cards worriedly. Cruella's sister, Rosa is the one doing all the laundry. I guess you could call her the laundress. Rosa appears occasionally carrying stacks of fresh, folded white towels from down the hall. She is smaller and darker and definitely more pleasant than Cruella, but we hardly ever see her.

Today´s topic in the common room is Fashion. Aella Mara and Nurse Ratched and a patient I have not noticed before, who is memorable only for her coat, talk about outward-facing seams on mock-shearling coats that are currently the trend. They examine the coat behind me, brushing it back and forth across my back and hair as they hold it out and examine it. This goes on for five minutes. I slump forward to try and give them more exhibition space.

The man who looks like Kermit the Frog is José. Today José makes a joke. As Nurse Ratched pats his shoulder in passing, José brushes off his shoulder in a very theatrical, mock disgust. This is all done silently, but I laugh out loud. The young athlete across the room in shorts and knee wraps looks up from his cot, looks around the room as if seeing us old folks for the first time, then he starts laughing. Soon, we are all laughing. Loudly, hysterically, for a long time. Laughing so hard that tears are rolling down all of our faces.

Aella Mara seems disgusted with me all the time now. She has become punishingly rough with (H), as if it´s my fault that (H) is slow to heal. She grudgingly allows me to have now what she calls "ice cream," in that sardonic, laughing way of hers, but she makes me beg for it. This is in a tall bottle of spearmint-colored lotion that has been added to my equipment assemblage. She adds a few drops to the Nivea cream. This makes her massages less painful, but still, I cannot help but wince and moan sometimes.

Laurinda stops inserting dowels into her board today. With both hands she draws tear tracks down each of side of her face. She speaks to tell me that when she first arrived, Aella Mara made her cry. I compliment Laurinda on her improved hand dexterity, and she blushes like a girl.

WEEK 5: Aella Mara has prescribed a new treatment for me - which I love! I now go straight back behind the curtain into the paraffin bath. (José has always gotten this treatment.) The melted paraffin is a bright electric blue in an insulated stainless-steel tank. I dip in my hand one, two, three, four times, counting to five between dips to allow the wax to cool and harden so the next dip will not melt it off. I grab one, two, three paper towels from the wall dispenser, wrap the paper towels around my hand, then take one of the two white towels hanging on the string that is stretched across the wall like a miniature clothes line. The towel insulates the warm wax. I go back to sit at our table.

Aella Mara has shown me how to do this, and occasionally she tries to squeeze into the wax cubby in time to hand me the towel. Being quick I avoid her, and return to Laurinda and José , my brother in arms. The three of us sit together silently enjoying the hushed murmur of the room before Aella Mara comes to massage H. Today I notice that under the grey plastic sheet is a fine, white cotton percale mat, hand-made with finely stitched corners folded down to hold the elastics at each corner that wrap around the table´s vinyl padding. The cloth has been starched and ironed.

The trees beyond the roof vent pipes glow like hope for the future. Most of us would be really annoyed with ourselves for getting older if it wasn't so pleasant being here. It´s cozy from the heat, and the clean smell of laundry. Yes, we´re aging. Yes, our bodies are failing, but we have each other. We are dying, but each day at 11 we encourage each other to live a little bit longer.

THE PORTUGUESE MODEL OF PHYSIOTHERAPY

Laurinda's father was Spanish. I'm reminded of guitarist Laurindo Almeida. (Researcher note: guitarist Laurindo Almeida was Brazilian.) Dowel-sorting is so painful for her that she stops often now to sigh, and to say a few words to me. I guess I'm getting better. In truth my facial muscles get as much of a workout as (H). This is a major improvement in my personality overall. (Researcher Note: Smiling was not considered an indicator in meeting the goals of physiotherapy.)

WEEK 6: We frequently mimic violence toward each other, pretending to snap off each other's limbs, and bite each other's necks. This is done with an unspoken understanding that it is a necessary tactic to prevent Nurse Ratched, Aella Mara and Rachel, (who, although sweet now, could easily be corrupted by the other two) from inflicting real violence. The therapists pretend not to see us. I think they are really scared of us.

Today I learn the name of the repetitive wall-washer is Leonor. She is not Brazilian, but

Portuguese. She comes over to point out that she and I are the only ones in the room at that brief moment. She is fifty-four. She has a twenty-nine-year-old daughter. She moves to her cot to begin her routine: lying on her tummy, moving a small dumbbell up and down her lower back. I realize what sets her apart from the rest of us is that she is naturally, wholesomely sexy. Literally anyone would have sex with her without a thought. The same cannot be said about any of the rest of us. I no longer think she works in a bar. I think she dresses lightly because she is just hot-natured.

Nurse Ratched's hiking boots are very nice quality. I tell her so, and ask if they are comfortable. She is really very pretty in a handsome way. Everyone discusses footwear for a while. Today two seagulls sat on the roof looking in at us, backlit by the golden trees. Usually, there is only one seagull.

WEEK 7: Christmas decorations went up after I left yesterday; decals of poinsettias, green garlands, and cellophane-wrapped candies dancing across the window top and the glass transom over the door to the blue curtained corridor. The candies look so real with the weak sun shining through that I crave sugar.

Cruella came back to the common room today to tell me that Dr. Nuno (not entirely his real name) has summoned me to his office. I feel nervous, also special. His desk is ancient brown wood. It nearly fills the room. He has a window with the same view as ours. There are three framed diplomas from Portuguese universities on the wall. "The hand is difficult," he says, reaching for mine, as he reaches back through time to English classes decades ago. "It has a mind of its own," he says. He wants me to stop coming to the *Clínica*. "I respectfully disagree," I say, bolstering my argument by reporting my hand is "so stiff," in the mornings and, "in really bad shape" after a weekend away. He is a sweet-natured, Old-World gentleman, and he agrees to let me continue. Because he said my tendons have been "overworked," and need a rest, I announce this to the waiting room group as,

"Doctora fala Aella Mara es muito violent! El fala es necessario para meu recover." I shake my finger imitating the doctor lecturing Aella Mara. Patrícia´s children look puzzled. Sandra´s husband, and the other patients chuckle.

WEEK 8: Cruella was not here all week. Rosa, has been assigned in her place. Tall, sleepy-eyed José now runs frantically back and forth, sometimes carrying laundry, and sometimes managing his index card case files. Leonor walks her fingers up and down a metal grid on the wall like the dance of fingers to the song, "The Itsy Bitsy Spider." Next, she moves to the block station in the corner. Margarida smiles her ironic, happy smile, (I see only her small chin and mouth where her welder´s shield stops.) She gives me her shoulder shrug, as she weaves between the stool and the toddler's mattress. I look up from taking notes on my iPhone to see Nurse Ratched has intercepted Margarida. They are dancing to Frank Sinatra singing, "Santa Claus is Coming to Town." Sandra lies on her cot, with her hands under her head, elbows splayed out, jiggling her two feet to the tune, looking like a girl on a beach on a summer vacation.

WEEK 9: My mobile phone is old, and often needs charging. Now all I have to do is hold it up to Cruella, and by the time I've come around to the other side of her desk she'll already have her charger cord out of the socket to let me plug in mine. Cruella came back to work today. She was not sick. She was in Mexico for ten days! She shows me picture after picture; her tall, pretty daughter, and her eight-year-old granddaughter. Cruella wearing a white, embroidered huipil looks *exactly* like Patrícia Arquette. All three look so relaxed and happy! Just imagine if every receptionist could take a 10-day holiday to the opposite side of the world! I tell her my bean tortilla recipe, which she writes down. To be warm here when it is cold outside, to be the focus of attention, even if painful, to be away from responsibilities for one hour every day, and to share this special time with each other is also a holiday.

WEEK 10: Laurinda tells me, "Meu tratamento está completo. Espero que o seu tratamento corra bem." She takes my hand in hers. "Está seu complete? Seu es finis?" I ask. She nods Yes. I am so happy for her. She worked so hard. I tell her this. She shakes her head with her endearing modesty.

(UNKNOWN WEEK:) Dr. Nuno wants to see me again after treatment. He informs me that I must allow my hand to heal on its own now. I am so stunned leaving his office that I do not question when Cruella tallies my bill for forty treatment sessions and asks for sixty-three euros - a total payment of sixty-three euros plus the initial fee of €13.75.

THE PORTUGUESE MODEL OF PHYSIOTHERAPY

It is that lonely time after Christmas when local friends are away on holidays, or have hands full with visiting family. This year my US family and friends have not visited because I am traveling to see them in March. (No travel happens due to the COVID-19 border closing precautions.) I pass between my *Clínica* friends nested snugly together like birds in a nest in the warm waiting area smelling of clean laundry. I descend the staircase for this last time. My knee hurts, as it hurts almost every time I go down stairs. This time the pain elates me! When I fell on my driveway two years earlier, I was covered by *Medis* insurance! I did not then know Dr. Pine Tree or his radiology ruffians, nor Cruella, Aella Mara, Dr. Nuno, Nurse Ratched, Rachel, José, or Rosa. Now, I know where to find them. It won't be the same though, without the old gang at my table, against the wall, in the corner, in the paraffin bath, and those I never saw, but whose particular moaning behind the blue curtains I´d know anywhere.

FURTHER DISCUSSION:

(Researchers Note: This may be a good place as any to fulfil the PS demand that *Medis* insurance be duly notified that she and H are available as company spokesperson and hand model.)

The APFISIO physiotherapy goals of "psychological, emotional, and social well-being," may seem overly ambitious. They did so to this Researcher, who comes from a country where less than half the workforce has any healthcare assistance at all, 30 million unemployed receive no healthcare, and healthcare expenses are the number one cause of bankruptcies. However, the Portuguese psychosocial physiotherapy goals align with the Hippocratic, Indian Ayurvedic, and Persian Yumani traditions, in which the body and the psyche are considered as one interrelated system. In addition, the Hippocratic tradition recognizes the impact of the socio-political environment on the health of the individual. Portuguese national policies prioritize equal access to healthcare, healthy natural foods, education, and even free entertainment. Portuguese life expectancy is also far above US life expectancy, which has been in decline since the 1980s.

The Primary Subject (PS) reported anxiety, and dislocation when treatment was "abruptly and unilaterally" completed. Empirical observation suggests the PS is prone to exaggeration, hyperbole, possible hypochondria, and even clinical psychosis, however research from the field of Trust suggests the PS may not be entirely *louco* (Portuguese medical jargon.) In a study of temporary workers in the film and theatre industry Meyerson, Weick, and Kramer find "swift trust," and intense attachment develop during relatively short, intense exposure to others when:

- Participants have a limited history of working together.
- Participants have limited prospects of working together again in the future.

- Tasks are often complex and involve interdependent work.

- Tasks have a deadline.

- Assigned tasks are nonroutine and not well understood.

- Assigned tasks are consequential.

This Researcher finds similarities between the patients at S & M Fisio and the temporary workers in the film and theatre industry studied by Meyerson, Weick, and Kramer.

Another study of trust in temporary groups by Dougherty found "the coming into existence of a special form, like a soccer match, conversation, or orchestra," in which participants' "perceptions are favorably enhanced, allowing for fresh thinking and discovery." Setting aside possible hypochondria, psychosis or simply an annoying personality on the part of the PS, the sense of loss and displacement she reported when "opportunities for discovery" were "abruptly and unilaterally" ended may be explained in part by such findings in the field of Trust. Whether a sense of loss and displacement has been reported by other patients at this physiotherapy practice, or at other practices in Portugal is beyond the scope of this study. But <u>if</u> such loss is found to exit, the solution may be as simple as a sandwich.

Portugal has a vast network of *confeitarias, padarias,* and *pastelarias,* often several to a single block, and these are clearly marked with no "misleading" posters. These establishments offer companionship, coffee, and snacks for as little as one euro, eliminating barriers to entry. Simple, low-cost modifications could enable *post-physiotherapy therapy*, better assisting the APFISIO´ psycho-social goals of "psychological, emotional, and social well-being" over the long-term. All that would be needed are a toddler's foam football, a tub of Rep Putty, wooden dowels, children's blocks, and a pair of nunchucks to be added to one small café table top in each establishment, provided by the good Republic of Portugal.

WORKS CITED

"A Fisioterapia em Portugal," Coutinho, Isabel Sousa e Pedro, Luísa, Fisioter. Pesqui. 25 (4), Dez 2018. https://doi.org/10.1590/1809-2950/00000025042018

"A Fisioterapia Cresce em Portugal," Vital, Emanuel, APFISIO, 16, Nov 2017.

http://www.apfisio.pt/fisioterapia-cresce-portugal/

"Swift Trust in Temporary Groups," Meyerson, Debra, Weick, Karl E. and Kramer, Roderick M., Trust in Organizations, Sage Publications, 1996. (Meyerson, 1996)

"Interpretive Barriers to Successful Product Innovation in Large Firms," Dougherty, Deborah. (1992). Organization Science, *3*(2).

FRANCELOS

Daneosa is a black boy aged twenty-two. At twenty-two he is still a boy. As Daneosa says, this is *No problem*.

Daneosa says *No problem* a lot. He speaks *un peau Francais, e un peau Anglais.* Of course, he speaks Portuguese.

Daneosa is working at the Apeadeiro Supermercado de Francelos. I was dropped off here—as it turns out, by mistake—because a thoughtful young woman gave detailed instructions to the *biologic market,* and this is where they led. She walked with confidence. She appeared bookish, artistic, perhaps a violinist, (an instrument one cannot play casually.) She was wearing an off-white stocking cap, a camel jacket, and hiking boots. She tread with purpose.

The Apeadeiro Supermercado is a corner store sitting pretty as can be on a slight hill across from the Francelos Train Station. The train station is adorable. Surrounded by a charming park, the whole spot looks like an idealized illustration from an antique children's story book, *Madeleine* or *Babar the Elephant.* Small scale, and dotted with camelia trees pruned like lollipops, the park has enough wrought iron benches for anyone who wants to sit and rest in this pleasant spot to sit and rest here. It might also be a miniature model train set train station. It is frozen in time.

I enter the shop excited, and eagle-eyed. I am looking for carrots, and any other organic vegetable or fruits I might find in the dim shop, and there is Daneosa. Tall and kinetic, he begins following me at once to understand how he might help, what it is that I might want. I try to ask the white woman sitting behind the meat case. Static and older, she seems managerial, despite her asymmetrical, butch haircut. Daneosa comes forward, instead. At first, he uses his phone translation application to talk to me. Then, because I am just here for vegetables and not a language lesson, we just use ourselves. This application of pointing with fingers works perfectly. Also, words for foods I learned straight away to avoid starvation.

Daneosa is wearing black jeans and a black T-shirt. His teeth are very white. I cannot see his teeth because this is COVID, and he is wearing a blue disposable mask, but his eyes are very white, and he stands and gestures and walks with a happy, rolling gait, swinging his shoulders, and confident, so I know that he is smiling under the mask, and I´m almost certain that his teeth are very white.

The case in front of the static managerial woman has a few pre-packaged meats, and a few thick slabs of bacon lying on white squares of paper. The store is heavily stocked with non-perishables. A whole aisle is devoted entirely to shampoos on both sides. Another aisle is all cleaning products. I have found the small produce section. I stand before it with Daneosa straining at my elbow to assist. The legumes (that means all vegetables in Portuguese) have perished. I mean of course they are dead, but these also look dehydrated.

There are four stalks of *alho francês*, (leeks). These are always durable, and one should never make the mistake of trying to use these uncooked in place of scallions. There are six heads of cabbage. The cabbage looks ancient and withered. Its green leaves have been peeled back many times revealing unwholesome-looking, pasty white heads. A water-filled container of parsley is still perky. The broccoli crowns—two—have turned yellow, as have the four cauliflowers. The courgettes look fine, but I find courgettes insipid, uninspiring under the best circumstances, as when there are plenty of other supporting ingredients to make *ratatouille* or *minestrone*. There are six hopeful cucumbers here. That's it.

There is some discussion at the meat counter between the static woman and a shopper who has just entered. She is a large, soft-bodied woman with perfectly round plastic tortoise-shell eyeglasses and medium-brown hair falling just below her shoulders. Her hair has been crimped, as if slept on in braids. The woman is in her late forties. She says there *is* a biologic market. As the three of them - the manager, the soft-bodied customer, and Daneosa - discuss its location I look around to see if there is anything at all I could buy here. I have the nylon backpack my daughter brought back from Bilbao, Spain´s Guggenheim Museum shop years ago. It stays inside my new, Lancaster shopping tote, which stays pressed under my armpit.

The manager behind the meat case explains where the biologic market is. "está perto? (Is it close?)" I ask. "Sim, está perto, (Yes, it's close.)" answers the manager. The consulting customer agrees enthusiastically. "Do you want me to take you there?" asks Daneosa. (I am not sure what language he says this in.)

"OK," I say, assuming Daneosa will walk me to the door, and point the way. All three gesticulated toward the left, so I expect Daneosa will walk me to the door and point to the left. At most he will walk me outside a few steps, then point to the left. At the very most I think he might walk me to the end of the block.

We walk outside together intersecting a man cutting across the park diagonally. He has an interesting pinched face, with high cheekbones, oversized ears, and an alarmed and confused look. He sees us and gives us warm and meaningful eye contact, and a thumbs-up. The man is carrying a small, packaged edible cake. In another country in another time, I would say this is a package of Hostess Twinkies.

Daneosa turns to the right. "Let's go!" he says. He is striding ahead on his long black legs to a car, which is a completely black car. I mean, completely. He has already opened the passenger door for me, and he is already seated in the driver's seat.

All the silver normally on a car, the chrome trim, has been painted black on this car. I get in. The car is spotlessly clean. The seats are black vinyl, or more possibly, black leather. Because everything on the inside of the car has also been painted black, it is impossible to see what make of car this is. It too appears timeless, an American muscle car. Maybe it is a 1990s Ford Mustang that we are inside.

"OK," I say. The seatbelt is stretched all the way out. The shoulder strap loops on the floor. I put it on anyway. Daneosa waits for me to do this. "Let's go!" he says again when I have clicked the looping strap's buckle. He says this triumphantly in English. We begin this day's small adventure.

Daneosa is from *São Tomé e Príncipe*. I have never met anyone before from *São Tomé e Príncipe*. If the others from there are anything at all like Daneosa, I think I would like them. I think I´d like to go there soon. We are driving all around curves very fast, but I am 100 percent confident in Daneosa's driving ability. His car, for one thing, is impeccable. He would never let anything bad happen to it. We approach a scenic bridge overpass. Daneosa slows down as a red convertible Porsche pulls to a stop on the other side. "Hey!" yells Daneosa. The driver is a middle-aged white man, well-fed. He breaks into a delicious smile, the maple syrup poured on warm pancakes with butters already-melted smile. He yells back. They share a few paragraphs. We pick up speed again. I ask, "Do you know that man?" I am incredulous. Daneosa is an *estrangeiro*, a young one, and a black one at that. "Yes. He is a colleague," answers Daneosa in English.

Huge *planos* trees that are at least one hundred years old line the roads now. We pass in front of old houses. We come to a small roundabout. There, straight across the grassy center a faded, fragile-looking cloth banner droops between branches of an old tree. It looks like white cloth that was soaked in strong tea. The words "Biologic Mercado 50 Meters," are still readable. We turn down that street and creep three hundred meters, passing charming houses set back under old trees. He looks that way. I look this way, a system we've wordlessly worked out.

A woman is standing on a second-floor balcony. We stop in front of her house. I leap out of the car to explain, using my dog-like Portuguese. Daneosa backs me up in his elegant Portuguese, with his beautiful, hidden white smile. The woman looks remarkably like Isabella Rossellini. Her hair is cut short. She has large, beautiful eyes. She asks, "Would you like to speak in English?" "Yes, thank you," I answer. Behind the woman a pale face appears from darkness. Her mother? An elderly lover? A care client? The beautiful Rossellini directs us back two hundred meters.

Daneosa takes these by going forward the long way in more joyous swooping, around and down the hill of the land. I approve of this wholeheartedly. I never travel backward on general principle. We wind up in front of a small yellow house. "This is it," says Daneosa. I look out cautiously. There is a table at the back of the driveway. A woman at the table is wearing an apron. There are a couple of other people. A clean-cut young man comes toward us down the driveway. "No. This isn't a biologic market. This is my house," he says, "We had a new baby. My mother-in-law is visiting."

He points to a small sign on the other half of his house. The house is a duplex. The sign is blue and white azulejos. It reads *"Cooperativa Frutaria."* The house has that balanced, linear, mid century modernity. It appears to have been built in the 1950s. "It is just historic," says the man referring to the sign.

We return to the Apeadeiro. Not defeated, not at all. We are refreshed to learn that this is a town that shares the same dream. Each resident may dream of it slightly differently, and in a different location, even. But everyone in this town believes the *biologic frutaria* exists. They believe this with all of their hearts.

LOVE IN THE AIR

> *"Across the morning sky all the birds are leaving, but how can they know its time for them to go?"*
> Sandy Denny, Who Knows Where the Time Goes. Lyrics © Fairwood Music (UK) Ltd.

It´s never been all that difficult for me to leave a relationship. Leaving the US was the same thing. I try to be fair. I put a lot of myself into most things I do. When that´s not enough, I just go. I gave money for gun control, for political candidates, and volunteered in food coops, public radio, solar energy, neighborhood associations, public transit, Brownie Troop, Little

LOVE IS IN THE AIR

League soccer, PTA, School Governance Council, County Council Committee, church committees, housing policy, voter registration, election calling, school tutoring, anything I could think of to help out. When things still were not working out with America, I flew away. The aftermath of leaving a relationship has never been easy for me, though.

I arrived in Portugal in July 2017 broken-hearted. I was really stumbling blind. I clung to my cell phone like a rebound lover, stumbling down one dark, cobble-stoned alley after another, and back up into sunshine to please its navigation system, and nothing I ever did was right for it. Navigation systems don´t work in Porto. It may be the city´s density, its granite hills, and buildings made of granite confound satellites. Or, it may be the cartographers working for Google blow off the behemoth to sail instead over the Douro River to Gaia's wine cellars. And, who could blame them? It´s not as if getting lost in Porto is all that bad. The cartographers could look down drunk from the Teleférico happy, and content in their belief that no harm would likely befall their fellow human beings in the Third Safest Country in the World. For four years I had no car here. At first, I was always walking, and I was always lost, and always asking people on the street for directions. What happened is that I was often getting kissed.

The directions, when I received any, were rarely reliable, and in retrospect they may have been *apology kisses*. Other kisses must have been *sympathy kisses*, because I looked really bad. The noise from the sewage pipe replacement project outside my apartment kept me on the streets from seven a.m. until seven p.m. when the machines quit for the day. I had few changes of clothes, no working kitchen, and to conserve funds I ate just one real meal a day. I was becoming gaunt, and was haggard from sleeping on mattresses hard as granite in furnished apartments. Certainly, my hygiene was also affected. Even this smelly, old hag got Portuguese kisses.

There were *make-up kisses* after arguments due to my lack of understanding the language or the culture. These it turned out were easily resolved by dissolving into laughter, then kisses. There were *shopping kisses* after I entered stores looking for items common in the US, but wholly unknown to exist in Portugal, like boxed stationary in the stationary stores called *papelarias* that grace almost every block in Portuguese towns. I´d walk back out empty handed, and dazed, but tenderly face-cup kissed.

When I bought my own house without major construction outside, with a working kitchen, *frutarias*, *feiras* and grocery stores within a short walk, and a comfortable mattress, I must have looked tastier and the offers of kisses became more insistent. Whenever I called the plumber with the simplest yes and no question, like *Is the washing machine hooked up?* he showed up almost immediately bearing gifts of herbs from his garden. After I asked my Portuguese friend, Cláudia what an appropriate Christmas thank you gift to a valued tradesman might be, and he stood toe-to-toe with me expectantly after I gave him the bottle of whiskey, and *Bolo Rei* cake that she suggested, I realized that he had always wanted to give me more than his plumbing services. (Now that I think of it, Cláudia married a tradesman in gravel substrates.) The taxi cab drivers offered me "special services," on learning I was "alone." These may have been purely professional - add-on services like wine-tasting tours to sample local cuisine.

The cleaning service owner was a young man with a large melon-shaped head on a neck like a papery, long, dried vine. All the previous cleaners I´d tried had been referrals to somebody's aunt or mother who had not worked in decades, and was not about to start now. They all showed up with an apron that they put on with an elaborate ceremony accompanied by sighing. The aprons all had pockets. This is where they carried the bread rolls and cakes that they snacked on while strolling from room to room examining my curious, foreign things. There was not one person like this, there were four. Some were pawned off as "excellent," and even, "an angel" by British ex-pats assuming naturally a less-discriminating Yank would never know the difference. (Note to readers from the former British Empire: Americans can be discriminating. Some of us are unqualified snobs.) If the cleaners had brought sensible snacks like carrot sticks I wouldn´t have minded so much, but I had no vacuum cleaner, and they always forgot to bring theirs.

After two years of sweeping crumbs after the cleaners left, I was delighted to find this young man´s professional cleaning service. The man would drop off his two, young, energetic cleaners in a van. All came wearing uniforms, and with professional equipment. One of the cleaners was particularly sweet, and also, very pretty. The night that her boss spent six hours sending me romantic text messages was a turning point for me. Anyone who knows me will tell you that I am not a diplomatic person by nature. I exhausted all of my diplomacy, and apparently, I´d gotten too good, because the man then began hanging around with the cleaners, but doing manly things, like the day he spent four hours hosing down my driveway. When the better, and prettier employee quit in tears one day, saying that she was needed more hours at her fish market job, the other cleaner became positively slovenly and surly toward me. She threw the dirty door mats onto my white sofas, and she threw frequent references to her boss as her "boyfriend" into my face.

When my neighbor lost her job at the bakery because her boss wanted to divorce her, I thought I had the perfect excuse to get rid of the cleaning company and save the owner´s face. I told him that my neighbor needed the money more than he did. My neighbor had no interest in cleaning my house, no interest in helping my friend, Sharon with her childcare, and no interest in any of the jobs I found her. I think she had more of an executive cake-eating position in mind. The cleaning service owner got over me quickly, billing me €400 for the rest of our contract. But, Oh! What a relief it was to have a dirty house again!

I guess I´ve aged out. Offers of kisses have gotten fewer. I also bought a car, so rarely find myself anymore in those long, intimate rides with taxi drivers these days. But it´s still true a friendly-faced person in northern Portugal can barely walk a kilometer without at an offer of a kiss. Towns even include kissing in their municipal budgets, building gazebos called *namoradeiras* for kissing in scenic locations!

In the United States I went for years without a single offer of a kiss, and this was while I was married. For twenty-five years I lived in Charleston, South Carolina, which is considered such a romantic place that it is a popular "Destination Wedding City." Spanish moss dangles seductively from old-soul oak trees. Humidity makes everything looks hazy, as if viewed through a theatrical scrim, and it does wonders for the skin. People go around saying *Bless your heart*. This is a barbed insult.

Women outnumber men nine-to-one in Charleston. Its women's publication, *Skirt!* featured ads for cosmetic surgeries that I wish I did not know about, and public hand-holding seemed a territorial act. The couples were a certain type. Between their mid-twenties and mid-fifties, at least one in the pair would be dazzlingly attractive, or dressed in clothing meant to dazzle, and tottering on very high heels clinging to an indifferent-looking man. This was of course a practical matter, and if the indifferent-looking man had a beer belly - which often he did - it was all the better. One strategic yank could transform him to a fluffy landing pad when an old-soul oak tree reached up through the pavement to trip the ridiculous footwear.

Right away I noticed that the hand-holding couples in Portugal were more varied. They could be children, or octogenarians, and they included ordinary-looking people. Some of the people were frankly unattractive - at least their clothing was unattractive. It is common to see couples in Portugal walking hand in hand wearing clothing stained with gear oil from wind turbines, and blood from the slaughtering of chickens. In general Portuguese people are so highly intelligent, and versatile that they can do almost anything.

Most Portuguese people are also very attractive. It's the way they move. They move beautifully. Some Portuguese hand-holders are of course much more attractive than normal people. The actress, Daniela Ruah and the scientist-politician, Alexandre Quintanilha, (not a couple,) are Portuguese. People in Portugal just seem to hold hands because they generally like each other. Footwear is incidental. Dangerous foot wear is not a prerequisite for love in Portugal.

I like some people, but I love textiles, and my love of textiles introduced me to Portugal. I began shoplifting clothing at age 13. Beginning with delicate, AA-sized bras and panties on my last haul I was so brazen that I stuffed a purple jersey middy dress, a gay, patterned jumpsuit, a wide-wale, button-down corduroy skirt, and a pair of wide-legged, bell-bottomed jeans into the sleeves and down in the lining of a vintage curly lamb coat my mother dragged home from an estate sale before I quit shoplifting for good. This was crime of opportunity because the oversized coat from the 1930s reached my ankles, had enormous balloon sleeves gathered at the wrists, and its pink satin lining was ripped under the arms and pockets, making one continuous pocket. It amazes that me no one in Bamberger's department store ever gave me a second look, when I must have looked suspicious even by the standards of 1969. These days my foreignness in Portugal is a little like that coat, cocooning me as I try to move inconspicuously, taking the odd and beautiful things I see that I want to keep around me.

At this age my grandmother Little Dot taught me to sew on her New Home sewing machine, which her grandmother had taught her to sew on at the same age. The machine is like jewelry; a black enamelled brooch with flowers and vines in jewel colors and gold. It´s bobbin winder outside the machine is heart-shaped, and to wind thread on the bobbin, (which catches the top thread, securing the stitches, for those who don´t sew) I hold the thread out and away from the machine between thumb and forefinger, and watch tiny teeth trace the heart, reversing at apex and inner V, as my foot holds a steady pressure on the pedal.

The first thing I made on that machine was a dark blue, almost black wool "cape," shaped like a narrow coffin, and stitched all the way down to my ankles so that I could only walk in small, mincing steps. I made slits for arms too low in front and too small, so my arms could only poke out like puny, Tyrannosaurus Rex arms. This was during my brief Gothic phase when I listened to The Doors, and had a black and white poster of silent film star Theda Bara, so I took such inconveniences in stride, (small, mincing stride.) My next poncho was more successful; a loose, knee-length style I made for my mother in a shockingly expensive, hand-loomed Irish wool that I knew was authentic because it looked just exactly like oatmeal, something which real Irish people ate.

I´d never spoken to my Great Aunt Miriam before turning up unannounced on her doorstep before my 16th birthday. Within days she took me out shopping for fabrics. I knew my grandmother, and their brothers had played mean tricks on Miriam, once getting her so drunk on brandied peaches they found in their basement that she nearly fell off the second-floor balcony at their Rutherford, New Jersey home. Surviving childhood, Aunt Miriam had married a scientist. My grandmother showed me a sepia photo of the happy, tan couple leaning into each other in The Bahamas. They'd lived in Los Alamos, New Mexico before settling in Los Gatos, California, where Aunt Miriam started a rare dolls business called *Peniston's Miniatures*. At Christmas time boxes arrived to me in New Jersey from the unimaginably far off place called *California*.

It might as well have been *Bhutan*. California was that remote to me. Inside brown paper boxes tied up with string were cloth dolls with gentle faces painted on fine-textured material that felt warm to the touch, like human skin. I found this description of them in Susan Brewer's book, *Famous Character Dolls*:

> "The dolls were made by the Fleischmann family, who fled Czechoslovakia in 1938,

settling in Britain. They settled in Rustington near Littlehampton in West Sussex. Margaret Fleischmann was tragically soon widowed and had to find some way of making a living, so decided to make dolls. She registered the name *Old Cottage Toys* in 1939. At first the dolls were all cloth but by the early 1950s were made using a mix of PVA and latex rubber for the heads, which gave them a highly distinctive look. The heads were hand-painted and attached to jointed cloth bodies. Margaret Fleischmann designed the costumes, and much of the sewing was executed by outworkers. Old Cottage Toys continued production up until 1980."

The PVA and latex used for the heads and necks melted in fairly low temperatures, so surviving dolls stored in an attic may have a bashful look, their heads melted cocked to one side, looking down. One year Cinderella as the princess arrived in a powdered wig, quilted silver lame

hoop skirt, and smooth silver lame bodice.
Prince Charming wore an ice-blue jacquard
waistcoat under an ivory satin tailcoat. They had
stockings, and great shoes, and layered
underwear trimmed in lace, and all the clothing
was removable using mustard-seed sized buttons,
tiny hooks and eyes, and satin ribbons scaled for
nimble fingers of tiny servants. Another year,
The Little Goose Girl arrived wearing a coarse,
red wool shift tied at the waist with a burlap
rope. Her underwear was plain, unbleached
muslin. I was living at the time in my mother's
antique shop surrounded by fine old things. But
these dolls were new and clean and the only
things of value exclusively mine, and therefore
off-limits to be sold to her customers.

When I turned up in Los Gatos, California I was
a high school dropout, a casual drug
experimenter, and a cross-country hitchhiker.
Aunt Miriam calmly asked what my plans were
now, (having accomplished so much already.) I
said I was considering becoming a fashion

designer, and that was good enough for her! She whisked me around Los Gatos´ better fabric shops, where I selected a sturdy white cotton twill with raised multi-colored stripes, and a black cotton chintz with larger than life, red, McIntosh apples.

Shoving her patient husband, Heber and his reading materials aside, Aunt Miriam set up her sewing machine in the sunroom. After a few instructions, she left me alone, interrupting only for meals I recall as experimental casseroles with vaguely ethnic aspirations. The sarong and halter top sets I made were hopelessly crude. None of the posh boutiques that Aunt Miriam took me to wanted anything to do with them, though she stood by proudly as I made my sales pitches.

A year and a half later, I was studying at Missouri Valley College (by a miracle; a school guidance counselor named Mr. Koch.) Another package from Aunt Miriam arrived. Inside were two warm lap throws. I still have the small-scale, wool plaid in maroon, apple green, pink, and royal blue on ecru, edged in simple royal blue button hole stitch, now worn thin as tissue paper. I still have one of the stolen bell-bottom jeans´ legs, embroidered in college with the words "You never leave a place you love. Part of it you take with you, leaving a part of you behind."

In college I walked with my cafeteria pay along the highway to the Bargain Bin, which still exists in Marshall, Missouri, for its tables covered in bolts of colorful quilting cottons until I found just what I wanted to make the "Spinning Wheels" applique quilt top from a craft magazine also found at the Bin. Wispy white clouds on pale blue sky, circus yellow calico, carnation pink calico with maroon, tiny flowers, dark green and gold paisley, black with blue flowers, and a classic, red bandana print made the wheels on the quilt. My daughter took it to her college thirty-five years later.

I still have the bedsheets that I bought in Kansas City in 1982 on a visit to my old college classmate, Liz Montague. Liz had arrived at the small, backwater college fortyish, her hair strangely colorless, looking chopped off by garden shears, and with two teenaged children in tow. Liz anchored our little group of misfits. We hung out at her off-campus flat drinking cheap wine, and listening to jazz records as Liz conducted our conversations from an old arm chair surrounded by stacks of library books that she used as side tables, (and had probably all read.) It was me, barely back from the hitchhiking exploits, "G.I. Joe," an older, muscular, chain-smoking Italian veteran from Boston with a diamond earring, a gangly, quiet brown-haired boy, and Liz´ children sprawled between us on the floor, doing their homework. When I visited Liz a few years later she was a Kansas City lawyer. She took me proudly to her favorite store, Macy´s, where though I had no money, and hadn´t planned on buying a thing, the cheeky hot pink, orange, and purple blossom sheets practically leapt into my arms. Somehow I found the $25 they cost. They are as vivid today as they were then. When I look at them I see Liz, glinting green eyes, her small, crooked smile, her expressive hand gestures, and her story. The bedsheets hold the beauty of seemingly impossible dreams fulfilled.

The man I married flew into sputtering rages when I brought home sheets from Kmart. He accused me of being a "spendthrift," which made making my retort easy: *If you wanted a more financially-conservative wife, you should have married an Amish!* In retrospect, now that he was an engineer in Charleston, South Carolina I was possibly *too Amish* for him. I cooked, baked, sewed our daughter's clothing, and did not own a pair of tottering high heels. My one extravagance was buying Martha Stewart sheets and towels when on sale at K-Mart. My marriage failed, but Martha's sheets have held up splendidly for more than twenty-five years.

As I made my own money, first by selling Kushies cloth diapers, eventually by selling houses, when I had extra money, I invested it in textiles. Gradually, I became aware of Portuguese textiles. I spent hours lingering over lovingly-photographed "100% cotton, made in Portugal" matelassé bedspreads and cotton-fleece blankets draped over painted bedsteads and bannisters in the Linen Source catalogues that arrived, to my delight, free in the mail. When our daughter was six her big Christmas gift was a Portuguese flannel duvet cover from L.L. Bean, expensive even on sale. It is butter yellow with periwinkle flowers. I still have it. Before The Linen Source went out of business I bought a few of the matelassé bedspreads and cotton fleece blankets.

Little by little it dawned on me: This land of comforting textiles, this Old World where the Cottage Dolls had been made, and where the fairy tales of hope, charity and perseverance had been written was a real place, a real, living place where real people lived today. With its everywhere ocean, 10 rivers, beaches, mountains, and trees, non-GMO breads, and most important of all, an intact social fabric Portugal sold itself.

It was only after I arrived that I found the love in its air. Each morning, and again at dusk dozens of little birds gathered outside my bedroom window to sing, their hearts so brimming with love that they could not wait one minute past 5:45 to begin. *Passeriformes* are mousy brown birds with "relatively large brain and superior learning skills," according to *Molecular phylogeny of songbirds (Passeriformes) inferred from mitochondrial 16S ribosomal RNA gene sequences*. They may certainly be smart, but it´s the size of their hearts that gets me.

The more famous Portuguese birds are the tuxedo-tailed, white-chested *andorinhas* immortalized by cartoonist-ceramicist, Raphael Bordallo Pinheiro in 1896. They are admired for their habit of mating for life. When I mention *andorinhas* to sisters Bella and Cristina - one married, one divorced –they smack their hands derisively in unison. "Fair weather birds!" they snort. It´s true. *Passeiros* keep us company through the long winters in Northern Portugal. *Andorinhas* abandon us for warmer southern Europe, and Africa as soon as things get dreary, but they fly as a couple. This fascinates me. What are their secrets?

Paco and Lis celebrated their 50th wedding anniversary recently. Paco is from Viana do Castelo, the town famous for its vivid embroidery. In photos from the 1970s Paco is smiling, dark-eyed, with a fashionable shag haircut, wearing wide-brimmed hats with scarf bands. Jimmy Hendrix would have followed him to his tailor. Paco´s aunt made most of his clothing; flowery shirts, flowing bell-bottoms, and velveteen suit jackets. At 16 Paco was already working in London for the shirt-maker Chester Martin.

LOVE IS IN THE AIR

Lis is fair-skinned, wide-eyed, moon-faced; a flower child, "from the garden in England, Kent," as she puts it.

> "We met on the North Sea, and have since lived in the following countries together; England, Germany, Sweden, Portugal, Mozambique, Angola, Libya, and Malaysia—in five different decades! My husband-to-be had just had his briefcase stolen, where his passport was, and so had not been able to enter Sweden as planned. Instead, he was put in a cell, and deported back to the UK on the following crossing—where he met me! My birthday was a few days later and he sent me a gorgeous card. That was it! Maybe this is why I love the sea so much, too?"

Paco and Lis taught English around the world for the Swedish government, specializing in a method of instruction called *Suggestopedia*, developed by Bulgarian Georgi Lozanov.

"Basically, it involves getting fear out of the classroom, creating a relaxed and comfy environment, and using fun and positivity for learning languages quickly. Specially written, tailor-made texts were read to classical music, too," says Lis. Most often they worked together, but not always.

> "I lived alone in Angola for eight months, in Libya a year, and in Egypt for one month. Paco worked in Angola during the war, and our first trip to Mozambique was during the war. It is now ten years since the evacuation from Libya when troubles started. I was in Cairo just after the Tahrir Square protests, Mozambique '88–89, and again, 2004–2009. Libya 2008–2011, Malaysia 2011–2015, Angola 2015, Egypt 2016."

To a recent birthday dinner Paco wore a floor length tunic with an elaborate embroidered white breastplate. After returning from Africa, to a party he wore a Gambian mud print dashiki suit with a matching kufi hat. He wears red velveteen bellbottoms to restaurant lunches. In a recent photo Paco is shown on the roof of their house - painting, not posing for a fashion shoot - wearing a white lab coat. "Didn´t I tell you we worked when we were younger in mental health hospitals?" says Lis.

I couldn't possibly have remembered that. Where they are in the world today is impossible to keep up with. In just the last year they´ve been at their country and city homes in Portugal, (both modest,) in the North and in the South of Sweden, where they mainly raised their children, on an island in Denmark, in Barcelona, in São Tome, back to Portugal, back to Sweden, in Dubai, in the Seychelles, back to Portugal, back to Sweden, and now they are teaching in Norway for a month.

I have an easier time tracking Ruslan and Nataliya. They perched on a cliff overlooking the sea outside Porto 23 years ago, and stayed. Their romance began in Ukraine:

"One November evening my friend and I went to the cinema. There was a film with Patrick Swayze, *On the Crest of a Wave*. At that time few people went to the cinema; everyone watched films at home on videotape. There were 10 people in the hall. My friend met her two friends. I didn't pay attention to the guys, and it was dark. I was in awe of the movie! Perhaps then, seeing these big waves on the big screen I fell in love with the ocean.

For two weeks the guys came to our work. We worked in the Centro de Emprego, and all went after to a cafe to drink coffee and eat cakes. Then they all accompanied me home together. One day Ruslan came in alone, and we went together, just I and he. We went to the Snezhinka cafe. He took two coffees and two cakes. He told me about the army as I ate a cake. Then he offered me to eat his cake. It was only a few years later he would tell me that my nose was covered in cream as I listened to him with what I thought was an intelligent face.

I worked for three years in the legal department. The Soviet Union collapsed. Corruption and bribery began. When applying to study or work, connections and money for bribes were needed. I worked very hard, and prepared hard for admission to law school but alas…It was very annoying! I wrote appeals asking why my exam was passed perfectly well, but I did not enter. The dream of being a lawyer has remained a dream.

Ruslan and I met for almost a year, walking together after work. On weekends we went with friends to nature. There were bonfires and songs with a guitar. Ruslan offered to marry me, and in October the guitar players played a wedding. There was no money but I wanted to feel like a bride.

This is after all one time and for life! The dress was rented, the parents helped to organize the wedding. Then, everyday life of family life began. Almost all the money earned went to pay for a rental apartment. Ruslan worked three jobs, was a driver of a bank director, and worked as a security guard in two commercial firms at night. In addition, I came up with different ideas for making money. Second-hand shoes began to appear in Ukraine. We bought Nike, Adidas, Reebok sneakers, washed them, made them look decent, and resold them. Then, sheepskin coats and leather jackets were cleaned, tinted, and sold. Then he got the idea to sharpen hairdressing scissors. Several of my scissors were damaged while he learned.

In the end, for two years before leaving for Portugal he was the best sharpener in our city. He was known in all hairdressing salons. There was enough money to pay for an apartment, electricity, water, Maks' kindergarden. (Maks is their elder son, living in Portugal since childhood.) Sometimes we would arrange a party for ourselves; buy honey beer, and make pizza. I will never forget the taste of that beer and pizza! There were fun times! And, how we believed in Amway! 'We have found a dream!` We saw ourselves as diamonds! Climb out of this layer, by all means. We read and read presentations, held second meetings with various people from traditional business. We read many books; how to work with people, how to believe in a dream and make it come true. For the last money we went to seminars and bought training tapes. But at some point, we realized that Amway is good as an additional income, and we needed to have a serious main income. So, the idea came to Ruslan to go to Portugal."

I have noticed that couples who are generally happy with each other seem to "leak happiness" around them. It is as if their happiness is too large for just the two of them. It felt like that on the Sundays my ex-husband and I walked over to his grandparents' house to watch *Murder, She Wrote*. Ed and Lila sat so close on the sofa that Lila was almost sitting on Ed's lap. They held hands the whole time, and were beaming, radiating happiness around them. Individually they were OK to be around, but when they were together there was magic.

One of the Portuguese people I mentioned as more attractive than most, (Greek God-like,) is Alexandre Quintanilha. His partner, Richard was one of the first people I met after moving to Portugal. Richard has a sort of explanation for this phenomenon,

> "In any relationship that is a true marriage (and there are marriages that are not marriages, they are two people living

together), there is person A, person B, and marriage. There are three living beings in a relationship and you have to be very careful with the third living being: marriage itself. You have to appreciate, polish, pay attention, otherwise the relationship will end. We are both very aware of this." (This comment was made to Anabela Mota Ribiero, published in *Publico*, 11, November 2012 in a story entitled, *The Man I Love*.)

With couples like this, I am not a "third wheel," I´m a fourth. I get along perfectly with the marriage!

Friends have invited me to "pick a boyfriend" from among older gentlemen they know at a local golf club. But dragging around expensive equipment in hot sun on a boring field with no trees to swing a stick at a ball now and then is not something I have any interest in. I can think of a million things I´d rather be doing. And, I don´t think these men want my contributions to their geo-political discussions, (which I never start, by the way.) They just want to swing their sticks around. Which is perfectly fine. For them.

Maybe I am a heron, an American bittern. "The American bittern, like many other herons, is solitary and moves slowly and secretively through dense marsh vegetation. Bitterns are most active at dusk and through the night. If alarmed, a bittern will stand motionless with its bill pointed straight up and its body contracted. This habit gave the bird its regional names of sky-gazer, look-up and stake-bird. Bitterns that flush when startled give a nasal "haink" call and beat their wings rapidly as they take flight. Bitterns call most often in the spring. A loud, guttural "pump-er-wink" is usually heard at dusk and gets its booming quality from a specialized esophagus. This unique call has led to many other common names, including water-belcher, mire drum and thunder pumper."

Thanks so much, Connecticut Department of Energy and Environmental Protection. Bless your heart.

Maybe I´ll find the perfect man for me in the Portuguese textile trades, but maybe I´ll just stick to his sheets. I am happy living here. I don´t want to be greedy. Flying solo, it´s nice though to live where love is in the air.

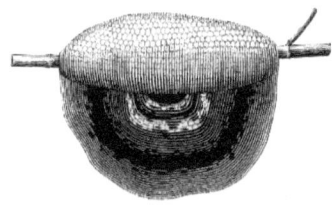

Portugal, On My Word

Oh, Portugal,

If I could take you in my arms and smother you with kisses, I would.

Your glaring, slinking cats.

Your stony stone.

Your stubbornness that refuses tyranny and fascism.

Your beautiful hills and swooning mountains.

PORTUGAL, ON MY WORD

Your scepticism, your earthiness, your common sense.

Your high intellect, your lowbrow cafes, your harbours.

Your mountain striders carrying flowers.

Your taunting ocean, your quiet small marshes, your fundamental farms

Your poets, your emigrants, your weavers of fabric.

Your laborers, your cobblers, your circus artists.

Your civil engineers, ceramicists, connivers and tall talkers.

Your secretive empregadas hourly scouring all things spic and span.

Your bland soups.

Oh, Portugal,

WEIRD FOODS OF PORTUGAL

If I could take you in my arms and kiss you -

Your frowning faces

Your glowering winter clouds

Your sun sweeping everything breathing gold
when the clouds roll out to sea.

You, with your fresh air, your edible fish.

You with your patient dogs, your sun-loving lizards.

You, with your trees so laden with fruit

branches are practically breaking begging

for relief.

Oh, Portugal,

Your trees relieved me.

I give you my heart, I give my mouth to nourish,

PORTUGAL, ON MY WORD

my hands to make wine and jams,

my feet to walk, to fall on your lumpy stones

on my knees - again and again –

Portugal, I give you my word, I love you.

Copyright 2021, Wendy Lee Hermance

Beijinhos

This book is a work of non-fiction. The persons and places mentioned in this book are entirely real. I might be all wrong about them, though.

Elsebeth Bull-Simonsen was always ready for our next adventure together. Bette passed away a few weeks shy of 88, disgusted at going so young. My old Sydney classmate and neighbor Mary Regan read all the way through my rough draft leaving positive comments highlighted in teal like exotic flowers brightening the dark forest of editing. David Rebelo helped edit "The Secret

Soldier," and told me to keep this section short. If you bought the first edition I´m sorry about that. My 12 year old laptop crashed at a critical moment and recovering the file I rushed editing. Sónia Cascais Sá volunteered to fix the "portuguese" for this new edition. Now it is as correct as Sónia, herself.

Andolino, António and Althea, António Soares, Ricardo, António, Conceição, and Elsa, Cláudia, Paulo Nóbrega, the residents of Quatro Caminhos Apartments – who I literally looked up to for guidance from my desk when I´d written something that didn´t make sense – all made me feel as if I might fit in and be OK here after all. I hope you enjoy meeting some of these people in these stories.

The Poetry Society of South Carolina, Charles Portolano of The Avocet, Francisca at Capela Inconum, A Casa da Boavista, Walter Bargen, Marjory Wentworth, Richard

Zimler, Joana Vasconcelos, and Rui Silvestre all gave moral support to my tentative writing. The John Wilkes Book Club at the British Council, and Carol Beth Whalen introduced me to new writers. All helped to write this book. Others just gave me material.

I am grateful to the Ministers of Portugal for deciding that since I´m as stubborn as a Portuguese person they might as well let me stay. To avoid any further misunderstandings the Ministers get only handshakes from me. Everyone else gets beijinhos.

Thank you for reading my books. If you like them, please write a review somewhere, and please share them with friends or frenemies.

Wendy

Aveiro, Portugal, November 2022

Serving as ballast to featherweight adventurer, Bette.

FURTHER READING

These writers, journalists, and performers help me think critically and stay unafraid to explore and enjoy our world.

I don´t agree with all of the views. But from where I´m sitting, where there is smoke, there is fire, and it´s probably a BBQ. I am going right over because I might finally find a vegetable side dish there, too.

1. *The Silk Roads: A New History of the World*, Peter Frankopan. Also, *The New Silk Roads*.
2. *Not in My Neighborhood: How Bigotry Shaped a Great American City*, Antero Pietila.
3. *Notes from the Edge of the Narrative Matrix*, Caitlin Johnstone. Also: https://caitlinjohnstone.substack.com/
4. *The Shock Doctrine*, Naomi Klein.
5. *Hate, Incorporated; Why Today's Media Makes Us Despise One Another*, Matt Taibbi.
6. *Confessions of an Economic Hit Man*, John Perkins.
7. *Unsheltered*, Barbara Kingsolver.
8. *The Feast of the Goat*, Mario Vargas Llosa.
9. *In the Distance*, Hernan Diaz.
10. *A Pattern Language: Towns, Buildings, Construction*, Sara Ishikawa and Christopher Alexander.
11. *Virtue Hoarders: The Case Against the Professional Managerial Class*, Catherine Liu.
12. *Bullet Points and Punch Lines*, Lee Camp. Also: https://www.youtube.com/c/MomentOfClarity, https://commoncensored.libsyn.com/
13. *Hunting Midnight*, Richard Zimler.
14. *Time Walked*, Vera Panova.
15. *America, the Farewell Tour*, Chris Hedges. Also: https://chrishedges.substack.com/

16. *The PayDay Report,* Mike Elk. https://paydayreport.com/author/mikeelk/
17. Cindy Sheehan, https://cindysheehan.substack.com/
18. *The Black Alliance for Peace.* https://blackallianceforpeace.com/
19. *The Expose UK.* https://expose-news.com/
20. *The Peoples Dispatch,* and *The People's Health Dispatch,* www.peoplesdispatch.org
21. *Mint Press.* https://www.mintpressnews.com
22. https://www.counterpunch.org/
23. *Children's Health Defense.* https://childrenshealthdefense.org/ Also: https://childrenshealthdefense.org/defender/ & https://live.childrenshealthdefense.org/
24. http://usefulidiots.substack.com
25. Kim Iversen. https://kimiversen.locals.com,
26. http://KimIversenemailsignup.comhttps://www.youtube.com/c/KimIversen
27. *Goliath: Life and Loathing in Greater Israel,* Max Blumenthal. Also https://thegrayzone.com/
28. Julian Assange: https://wikileaks.org/
29. *Informed Consent Action Network.* https://www.icandecide.org/support-ican/
30. *Lew Rockwell* https://www.lewrockwell.com/
31. Pam and Russ Martens. https://wallstreetonparade.com/
32. https://edwardsnowden.substack.com/

33. Glenn Greenwald. https://greenwald.substack.com/
34. https://www.russellbrand.com/
35. Jimmy Dore. https://www.youtube.com/c/thejimmydoreshow, And: info@jimmydorecomedy.com,
36. Matt Ehret. matthewehret@substack.com, And: https://matthewehret.substack.com/
37. Naomi Wolf. Naomiwolf@substack.com
38. Robert Malone. rwmalonemd@substack.com, And: https://rwmalonemd.substack.com/
39. CJ Hopkins. cjhopkins@substack.com

THANK YOU/OBRIGADO!

www.ingramcontent.com/pod-product-compliance
Lightning Source LLC
Chambersburg PA
CBHW060349080526
44583CB00012B/234